Short
CUTS

STEVEN SAUNDERS

MACMILLAN

First published 1998 by Macmillan General Books
an imprint of Macmillan Publishers Ltd
25 Eccleston Place, London SW1W 9NF
and Basingstoke

Associated companies throughout the world

ISBN 0333 71783 X

9 8 7 6 5 4 3 2 1

A CIP catalogue record for this book is available from the
British Library.

Design by Roger Daniels
Jacket design by Macmillan General Books Design Department
Photography by Philip Wilkins
Printed by New Interlitho, Italy

ACKNOWLEDGEMENTS

This book required a lot of planning and testing to get the
step sequences and timings right. This in turn made the
photography quite complex, so thank you to Philip Wilkins
for being so patient. It also made the editing very difficult,
so my thanks to Judith Hannam for putting up with this.
Many thanks go to Gordon Wise for his additional editing
and rewriting, and for helping me to create the book in the
first place.

My thanks also go to my personal assistant, Julie
Seymour, who typed the whole manuscript so brilliantly,
and to my mother, Joy Saunders, for thinking up the title.

Thanks are also due to Sally, for keeping me out of the
house for three months so that I could actually write this.

Contents

Introduction

Good food needn't take hours of preparation or standing over a hot stove. You have only to look at the innovative brasserie-style menus now being cooked all over the country to see that good food can happen quickly, and that simple techniques can often be just as effective as more complex, time-consuming methods.

Short Cuts has been written with this view very much in mind. I have created 90 chic and speedy recipes for four people (scale quantities up or down accordingly), put together in three-course menus assembled so that each dish complements the other perfectly. Some of the flavours are perhaps a little adventurous, but they are always classic combinations never the over-the-top concoctions you find in some books or on some television shows – sometimes I wonder if these dishes have actually been tried and tested. All I can say is that as a restaurateur this is the kind of good food that both my customers and I seem to enjoy.

Even though these recipes are put together in threes, do not be deterred from using one or two on their own, or from making some substitutions. Each menu is written in such a way that it's very easy to pick out the dishes you might want to prepare separately.

I hope you both enjoy and gain confidence from this book. It should encourage you to be a bit more adventurous, knowing that these are all tried and tested methods. And, above all, remember that the meals don't have to be cooked in such a short space of time – but if you do follow the recipes carefully, you'll have more time to socialise or spend in the garden!

Good luck,

STEVEN SAUNDERS

Timings

Assuming you follow the guidelines with each recipe, the actual cooking time for each of the three-course menus in this book shouldn't be much more than 20–30 minutes. This is not to say that to achieve this there isn't some preparation involved (see below), but you should be able to be in and out of the kitchen in well under an hour, unless you stagger things a bit more. You'll also obviously want to 'stop the clock' to serve, eat and enjoy each course, but look at all the steps first so that you can set things up for the next stage beforehand.

Although speed is the keynote of this book, don't make the mistake of thinking that it's a case of 'beat the clock'. That's fine for TV game shows, but not what really enjoyable cooking is all about. None the less, I've tried to simplify things so that they are manageable in the sort of time you're likely to have available to you.

The timings are designed to give you some idea of how long each step should take. Don't take them too literally; some of the dishes may take you a little longer, and some of the cooking times will vary according to taste, too. Timings are almost impossible to judge accurately because everyone works in different ways, and with different equipment. But you should find that once you have followed a complete menu through at least once, you'll be able to turn it out again and again a lot faster.

Equipment

All the menus can be easily created providing you have a standard stove with four burners or electric rings and an oven, and perhaps a microwave for really speedy results on a couple of the puddings. Each menu has an equipment list so that you are not caught halfway through a recipe without a vital tool. But for the most part these are very standard items; I just want to make sure you know in advance how many bowls and pans, etc. you will need. The lists are there to help you to pre-plan a little and not waste time looking for a utensil when you can have everything at hand before you start. I have for the most part omitted the very obvious, such as wooden spoons and kitchen knives.

On the subject of knives, I always use Drizakwerk or Gustav Emil Ern top-quality German stainless steel knives. They are available from most good cook shops or catering outlets. Global knives (Japanese stainless steel) are also very good, but more expensive, and a bit flashy! But remember that a good knife will stay sharper for longer and truly last, and is indispensable for any serious cook.

Ingredients

These should always be fresh, preferably organic, and seasonal where possible (for instance, don't attempt a fresh strawberry dish in the winter, as the fruits won't be at their best). Most of the ingredients I've used in this book are easily obtainable at a big, quality supermarket, or for a few things, a good delicatessen. They should all be affordable, even if sometimes a bit 'special'. I have recommended substitutes for ingredients that are more lavish or a little more difficult to find.

Preparation

Each menu has a few steps of pre-preparation per course. This is to help you get organised in advance, and be sure that the indicated timings are achievable. In some cases, you could prepare even more than I've suggested (such as when serving a cold starter or dessert) thereby reducing cooking time even more. Pre-preparation is an essential part of a professional kitchen's routine, and this book is in many ways inspired by that 'chef's secret'. We call it *mis-en-place*, and it may even include pre-blanching or -cooking vegetables, and pre-sealing meats for simply finishing off before serving.

When you add up all the preparation timings for each dish the process may look a little lengthy, but remember that while one thing's going on (for example, potatoes boiling) you can be getting on with something else. There's lots of scope for using the overlapping time.

You'll obviously also want to use your common sense; when I say to heat a pan or wok up in advance, this is to ensure that it's ready to go before you start cooking. I don't mean that it should be smoking at the back of the stove for ten minutes while you chop, whip or blend something else! This would clearly be very dangerous, especially if there is fat or oil involved. But the idea is to be a step ahead of yourself; if you'll need a hot pan in a minute or two, warm it up now.

Bear all this in mind at your planning stages. The more preparation you are able to do, the less time you will need to spend in the kitchen, which means more time at the table with your guests.

Stocks and Sauces

I could write at length about the fine craft of stock and sauce making. But *Short Cuts* is all about the speedier alternatives to lengthy cooking procedures, so although I always make my sauces up from fresh stocks in my restaurant (a few basic recipes for which I've included below) I often speed up the process at home and when I'm cooking on TV by using stock cubes as a base, and enhancing the flavour a little.

I tend not to use beef stock cubes, but instead use a vegetable stock cube with a little yeast extract (such as Marmite) to bring out a fuller, richer flavour. Never season a stock made from a cube until the last moment as they usually already contain a lot of salt.

QUICK 'MEAT' STOCK

1 vegetable stock cube
½ tbsp yeast extract (e.g. Marmite)
150 ml/5 fl oz water
150 ml/5 fl oz red wine

Combine all the ingredients together in a saucepan and reduce by half over a medium-high heat.

QUICK LAMB STOCK AND QUICK CHICKEN STOCK

Make as above but substitute either a lamb or chicken stock cube as required.

NAGE OR CLASSIC VEGETABLE STOCK

2 onions, coarsely chopped
1 leek, coarsely chopped
3 celery stalks, coarsely chopped
4 carrots, coarsely chopped
1 whole garlic head, cut in half horizontally
2 lemons, thickly sliced
1.5 litres/2½ pints cold water
6 black peppercorns
6 pink peppercorns
2 star anises
coriander sprig
tarragon sprig
250 ml/8 fl oz dry white wine

1 Place the chopped vegetables, garlic and lemon slices in a large saucepan. Add the water and bring to the boil.
2 When boiling, add the herbs and spices. Remove from the heat and let the flavours infuse for a few minutes. Add the white wine.
3 If you need to use immediately, sieve before use. For best flavour, however, pour the mixture into a large, clean container and let all the flavours infuse for two days or so in the refrigerator. When required, pass the

nage through muslin through a sieve, discarding the solids.

CLASSIC FISH STOCK

1 medium onion, peeled and sliced
1 leek, roughly chopped
½ head celery, roughly chopped
1 garlic clove, peeled and crushed
A little olive oil
250 g/8½ oz fish bones (large ones broken into smaller pieces)
125 ml/4½ fl oz dry white wine
125 ml/4½ fl oz double cream
250 ml/8 fl oz cold water, or to cover

1 Sweat the vegetables in a little oil in a deep saucepan, but do not allow them to colour.
2 Add the fish bones and stir in. Cover with water.
3 Pour in the white wine and reduce a little, simmering for about 30 minutes.
4 Add the cream and reduce for a further 5 minutes.
5 Pass through a fine sieve into a clean container, holding back any bones.

Note If freezing, sieve and do so when cool after stage 3, adding the cream when reheating.

QUICK FISH STOCK

1 fish stock cube
150 ml/5 fl oz water
100 ml/4 fl oz dry white wine
100 ml/4 fl oz double cream
Salt and freshly ground black pepper

Combine all the ingredients except the cream in a saucepan and reduce by half over a medium-high heat. Add the cream, reduce again over a lower heat for 5 minutes, then season according to taste.

VEAL JUS (for use with all meats)

3 kg/6½ lb veal bones
2 tbsp honey
2 carrots (whole)
1 onion (halved)
2 celery sticks (whole)
1 small leek
3 garlic cloves, peeled
200 g/7 fl oz can tomatoes
375 ml/11 fl oz red wine
1 tsp tomato purée
Salt and freshly ground black pepper

1 Preheat the oven to 230°C/450°F, gas mark 8.
2 Either have your butcher break the veal bones into small, manageable pieces or do this yourself. Place them on a large baking tray and roast in the oven, basted with the honey, for about an hour until golden brown.
3 Tip the roasted bones into a large saucepan, add all the vegetables with the purée and seasoning, cover with cold water, and bring to the boil.
4 While boiling, skim to remove the scum and then simmer for four hours, or until reduced by half.
5 Remove the bones and pass the liquid through a sieve into a clean saucepan.
6 Add the red wine and reduce for an hour.
7 Pass through a sieve lined with wet muslin to ensure that all impurities are removed. Allow to cool, then reserve in the fridge in a sealed container until needed. Remove any fat before reheating.

Note For a real chicken stock, substitute 3 kg/6½ lb chicken bones and dry white wine, and add a few mushrooms. For a lighter stock, boil the bones rather then roasting them.

GRIDDLED FRESH TUNA

with

FILO PASTRY AND BASIL OIL

CURRY ROASTED PORK

with

LEMON COUSCOUS AND

ROASTED ROOT VEGETABLES

POACHED STRAWBERRIES

with

PINK PEPPERCORNS AND

PISTACHIO ICE CREAM

**Total cooking time for 3 courses
approximately 18 minutes and
preparation time 18 minutes**

Left: Curry Roasted Pork with Lemon Couscous and Roasted Root Vegetables

These are three of my very favourite dishes. Fresh tuna is absolutely delicious, and so very different in flavour from the tinned variety. It's available nowadays from most fishmongers and supermarkets, although you may want to give a day or two's notice. Remember to keep it nice and pink, if not rare, to maintain its moistness and tenderness. If overcooked, it can be leathery. Further, the combination of fresh tuna with basil and filo is superb. If you're not a tuna fan, or can't find it, use your favourite fish instead. Salmon and monkfish will work well.

By tossing the pork fillet in curry powder before searing and roasting it you will get the most magnificent curry flavours without them being overpowering. Couscous is a delicate accompaniment, and works well under most meats and fish. Roasted vegetables always look and smell great, and are absolutely delicious.

Finish all this with poached strawberries and pink peppercorns (which give them a bit of spice), and you have a magnificent menu that can be ready in no time.

For the Tuna

INGREDIENTS

450 g/1 lb fresh tuna loin
2 sheets filo pastry (approximately 30 × 25 cm/12 × 10 inch)
55 g/2 oz unsalted butter, melted
1 tsp dried chilli seeds
1 large bunch (or 1 plant) of fresh basil
150 ml/5 fl oz extra-virgin olive oil
A little vegetable oil
Salt and freshly ground black pepper
Juice of ½ lemon
8 slices of sun-dried tomatoes (halves)

EQUIPMENT

Pastry brush
Pastry cutter (7.5 cm/3 inch diameter)
Baking tray
Food processor
Griddle
Palette knife

PRE-PREPARATION

• Carefully unwrap the two sheets of filo pastry, brush the first layer with the melted butter and place the second sheet on the top. Brush this with butter too, and sprinkle with dried chilli seeds.
• Cut into 12 × 3 inch/7.5 cm rounds, place on a baking tray and bake in a hot oven, preheated to 190°C/375°F, gas mark 5, for 3 minutes. Remove and allow to cool.
• Meanwhile, cut the tuna into 8 small 1 cm/½ inch thick slices.

 6 minutes

For the Pork

INGREDIENTS

2 × 225 g/8 oz pork tenderloins
2 large carrots
2 parsnips
2 large potatoes
3 dsp mild curry powder
A little vegetable oil
1 tbsp chicken stock
½ tsp yeast extract (Marmite)
175 ml/6 fl oz red wine or medium sherry
1 dsp caster sugar
Salt and white pepper
Sprig of fresh rosemary (or 1 tsp of dried)
150 g/5½ oz couscous
Juice and zest of 1 lemon
200 ml/7 fl oz vegetable stock (or water)
3 tbsp double cream or 55 g/2 oz butter

EQUIPMENT

Filleting knife
Chopping knife
Heavy based frying pan or griddle
Small saucepan for pork sauce
Whisk
Roasting dish
Small saucepan for couscous

PRE-PREPARATION

• Trim the fillets, if necessary, to remove the sinew and skin on top using a sharp filleting knife. Cut both fillets in half to produce 4 small fillets.
• Peel and prepare the vegetables for roasting.
• Preheat the oven to 200°C/400°F, gas mark 6.

4 minutes

For the Strawberries

INGREDIENTS

450 g/1 lb fresh strawberries
55 g/2 oz unsalted butter
55 g/2 oz caster sugar
100 ml/4 fl oz water
25 g/1 oz pink peppercorns
    (NB not black or green)
A little freshly ground black pepper
4 portions of pistachio (or similar) ice cream

EQUIPMENT

Medium saucepan
Measuring jug
Ice cream scoop
Whisk
Wooden spoon

PRE-PREPARATION

• Halve the strawberries and hull them (remove the cores).

8 minutes

Left: Poached Strawberries with Pink Peppercorns and Pistachio Ice Cream

Toss and roll the pork fillets in the curry powder to lightly coat; heat the heavy frying pan.

1 minute

Put the chicken stock and yeast extract together in a small saucepan, add the red wine (or sherry), bring to the boil and simmer until needed.

1 minute

Now fry (sear) the fillets so they brown evenly, using a little vegetable oil.

1 minute

Remove the pork fillets, place in a roasting dish and roast in the hot oven for 10 minutes.

1 minute

Meanwhile, pour a little more vegetable oil into the pan used to fry the fillets and sweat off the carrots, parsnips and potatoes, adding the sugar, seasoning and rosemary.

2 minutes

Keep the vegetables on the move in the pan so they colour but don't burn, then put them in the roasting dish too, and roast until tender, for approximately 7 minutes.

1 minute

Place the couscous, lemon juice and vegetable stock in the small saucepan, bring to the boil, then simmer for 2 minutes on a low heat.

2 minutes

CONTINUED

Now that everything is on the go for the main course, turn your attention to the tuna and strawberries.

Firstly blend the basil and olive oil in a food processor to create a basil oil and heat up a griddle pan.

1 minute

Sear the tuna pieces on the smoking hot griddle pan, with a little vegetable oil and season well. Add the lemon juice. Cook for 30 seconds on each side, turning with the palette knife, remove and allow to rest.

Serve the tuna in between layers of the prepared filo with the sun-dried tomatoes (as in the photograph on page 11) and the basil oil around.

3 minutes

Remove the pork and vegetables from the oven. Keep warm if you are not ready to serve. Check the seasoning and consistency of the sauce (it should coat the back of the spoon). Whisk in the butter or cream, taste and season.

1 minute

Serve the couscous in the centre of the plate with the sliced pork fillet on top and the sauce around.

1 minute

Start the strawberry dish by melting the butter and sugar in a saucepan, whisking in the water after 1 minute.

1 minute

When you are ready to serve the dessert, add the pink peppercorns and the strawberries to this warm mixture, season with a little black pepper, and poach for 1 minute, stirring with a wooden spoon.

1½ minutes

Serve the strawberries in individual bowls with a scoop of ice cream in the centre of plenty of sauce.

1 minute

S E A R E D   S C A L L O P S

with

R O C K E T   A N D   L A M B ' S   L E T T U C E

S U K I Y A K I   S I R L O I N   O F   B E E F

with

C H I N E S E   R I C E   N O O D L E S

C R I S P Y   M A N G O

T A R T S

**Total cooking time for 3 courses
approximately 15 minutes and
preparation time 13 minutes**

Although they can be expensive, if you can get hold of fresh, dived scallops you'll certainly taste the difference. Frozen scallops tend to be full of water, so when they cook they end up being poached really instead of fried, and, since they shrink as the water evaporates, you may find you have to use more of them, making them a false economy too!

Rocket and lamb's lettuce salad is in my opinion the perfect combination of green leaves, but replace them with leaves of your choice if they are hard to find.

The Japanese flavours of a sukiyaki sauce work beautifully with beef. And the crispy mango tart is a perfect marriage of exotic fruit flavour with fine, crisp pastry.

Right: Seared Scallops with Rocket and Lamb's Lettuce

For the Scallops

INGREDIENTS

3 large or 5 small scallops (out of the shell) per
  person
200 g/7 oz rocket leaves, approximately
150 g/5½ oz lamb's lettuce
1 dsp olive oil
Salt and freshly ground black pepper
A little vegetable oil
185 ml/6½ fl oz sweet white wine
1 fresh coriander plant
25 g/1 oz unsalted butter

EQUIPMENT

Bowl for salad leaves
Frying pan
Serving bowl or plate

PRE-PREPARATION

- Count out 4 portions of scallops, clean off any grit.
- Mix the salad leaves with the olive oil and season.

2 minutes

For the Beef

INGREDIENTS

4 × 200 g/7 oz sirloin (entrecôte) steaks
2 red chillies (fresh)
2 green chillies (fresh)
2 garlic cloves
Fresh root ginger or Galangal Thai ginger
4 spring onions
3 tbsp rice vinegar
100 ml/4 fl oz light soy sauce
Salt and freshly ground black pepper
A little vegetable oil
150 g/5½ oz fine Chinese rice noodles
1 tsp curry powder
Small bunch fresh coriander

EQUIPMENT

Bowl for marinating beef
Saucepan for blanching noodles
Griddle pan
Baking tray
Wok for noodles
Saucepan for heating marinade
Wooden spoon or spatula

SEE OVER FOR PRE-PREPARATION

For the Mango Tarts

PRE-PREPARATION

• Prepare the marinade: de-seed the chillies and finely chop, flatten the garlic with the blade of a knife and then finely chop, shred the root ginger and spring onions and mix together with the rice vinegar, soy sauce and seasoning.

• Place the beef in the marinade until needed (for an hour, if you can, but no more than 12 hours!); cover and place in the fridge.

• Bring a saucepan of water to the boil.

5 minutes

INGREDIENTS

225 g/8 oz puff pastry
A little flour for dusting
2 medium-sized mangoes
55 g/2 oz unsalted butter
115 g/4 oz caster sugar
150 g/5½ oz clotted cream to serve

EQUIPMENT

Rolling pin
Fork to prick the pastry
Sharp knife
Baking tray

PRE-PREPARATION

• Roll out the pastry to a thickness of approximately 3 mm/⅛ inch on a surface lightly dusted with flour and, using a side plate roughly 12 cm/4¾ inches in diameter, cut out 4 rounds and place them on to a baking tray.

• Prick the discs all over with a fork to prevent the pastry rising.

• Peel and thinly slice the mango and arrange on the pastry disks.

• Preheat the oven to 200°C/400°F, gas mark 6.

6 minutes

SEE OVER FOR METHOD

Heat the frying pan for the scallops and your griddle for the beef.

½ *minute*

Melt the butter for the mango tarts in a small saucepan (or a microwave), spoon a thin coating on to the pastry rounds, then sprinkle on the sugar. Place in the hot oven for about 10 minutes.

2 *minutes*

Meanwhile, remove the beef from the marinade. Pour a little vegetable oil (about 1 dessert spoonful) on to the hot griddle, sear a steak for approximately 30 seconds each side, and place on the baking tray. Repeat the process with the remaining 3 steaks.

2 *minutes*

Place the baking tray in the oven, and at the same time check that the mango tarts are cooking nicely.

½ *minute*

Pour a trickle of vegetable oil into the hot frying pan, then sear the scallops on both sides to give them a good colour, approximately 2 minutes.

1 *minute*

Now de-glaze the pan with the sweet wine and turn the heat right down to a gentle simmer, allowing the wine to poach the scallops for 1–2 minutes, then remove from heat and rest in liquor.

1 *minute*

Meanwhile place your wok (or frying pan) on a low heat. Place the noodles in the saucepan of boiling water, blanch them for 2 minutes, then remove and refresh under cold water. (Meantime, whilst waiting for the noodles, check the beef and the mango tarts, and start to bring the Sukiyaki beef marinade liquor to the boil.)

3 *minutes*

Pour a little oil in the wok, add the noodles, curry powder and coriander leaves, remembering to stir them well, and fry gently on a low heat.

1 *minute*

Meanwhile, remove the beef and allow to rest on a board. If they are to sit for a while, cover with aluminium foil to keep warm. Remove the mango tarts.

1 *minute*

Remove the scallops from the pan and serve in individual bowls with the leaves in the centre and garnished with coriander. Pour some of the liquor into each bowl. (If more juices are needed, whisk in a little melted unsalted butter and wine.)

1 *minute*

When ready to serve, cut the beef into 3–4 slices per portion, arrange on the noodles, and pour the (now boiling) Sukiyaki marinade over each portion.

1 *minute*

Serve the mango tarts warm with the clotted cream.

Left: Sukiyaki Sirloin of Beef

MENU 3

ARBROATH SMOKIES

with

POTATO SALAD AND

ROASTED CHERRY TOMATOES

———

ABERDEEN ANGUS FILLET

with

NEEPS AND WHISKY JUICES

———

DRAMBUIE ZABAGLIONE

**Total cooking time for 3 courses
approximately 25 minutes and
preparation time 15 minutes**

These three dishes are heavily influenced by the rich, traditional flavours of Scotland. Arbroath smokies are superbly-flavoured, smoked fish, and should be available from your fishmonger with a little notice. Aberdeen Angus is a free-range beef, and the only kind I serve in my restaurant. And what more need I say about the delights of whisky and Drambuie?

For the Arbroath Smokies

INGREDIENTS

4 smokies (see your fishmonger)
250 g/8½ oz cherry tomatoes
Bunch of chives
Salt
8 small whole new potatoes in their skins
Olive oil
100 ml/4 fl oz double cream
1 tsp English mustard
Nutmeg
Sprig of rosemary
1 dsp mayonnaise
A little cooking oil

EQUIPMENT

Knives
Saucepan for the potatoes
Saucepan for the cream
Frying pan
Glass bowl
A 7.5-cm/3-inch pastry cutter
Wooden spoon
Grater for the nutmeg

PRE-PREPARATION

• Remove the fish from the bone.
• Cut the tomatoes into quarters.
• Chop the chives.
• Bring a saucepan of salted water to the boil.

5 minutes

For the Aberdeen Angus Fillet

INGREDIENTS

4 × 225 g/8 oz fillet steaks
2 medium swedes
150 ml/5 fl oz beef stock
¼ bottle of red cooking wine
Salt and freshly ground black pepper
A little cooking oil
55 g/2 oz unsalted butter or créme fraîche
Nutmeg
75 ml/3 fl oz whisky

EQUIPMENT

Sharp knife
Saucepan for the stock
Griddle
Baking tray
Potato masher
Grater for the nutmeg
Wooden spoon

PRE-PREPARATION

• Combine the stock and red wine and reduce the amount of liquid by half on a high heat.
• Meanwhile, peel and cut the swedes into 1-cm/½-inch pieces. Place in a saucepan, cover with cold water and season well.
• Trim the steaks, if necessary.
• Place the griddle on a high heat.
• Preheat the oven to 200°C/400°F, gas mark 6.

5 minutes

For the Zabaglione

INGREDIENTS

100 ml/4 fl oz double cream
10 egg yolks
1 dsp water
85 g/3 oz caster sugar
100 ml/4 fl oz Drambuie (reserve 50 ml/2 fl oz for
  the bottom of each glass)
20 small amaretti biscuits

EQUIPMENT

Whisk (or electric beater)
Bowls
Saucepan large enough to accommodate
  1 of the bowls
Saucepan for the Drambuie
Glasses

PRE-PREPARATION

• Whip the double cream until it reaches ribbon
stage.
• Bring some water to the boil in the saucepan that
will accommodate the bowl.

5 minutes

Cook the potatoes until tender in a little water with
a dash of olive oil – this will take approximately 20
minutes.

1 minute

Meanwhile, bring the swedes to the boil, and cook
for 15 minutes.

1 minute

Proceed to coat the steaks in a little oil and sear on
both sides on the hot griddle.

1 minute

Place the beef on a baking tray and roast in the hot
oven for approximately 8–10 minutes for rare and
12–15 minutes for medium to medium rare.

1 minute

Combine the unwhipped double cream with the
mustard in a saucepan and reduce until thick. Add
the Arbroath smokies, stir in well, season with
grated nutmeg, and leave on a low heat.

2 minutes

In a hot frying pan with a little oil, sear the quarters
of tomato, skin side down, then place on a roasting
tray, with the rosemary, and roast in the oven for 5
minutes.

2 minutes

Check the wine sauce for seasoning and consistency
(it should coat the back of a spoon). Meanwhile
start the pudding.

1 minute

CONTINUED

27

Whisk the egg yolks with the water and sugar in a bowl placed over the saucepan of simmering water. (The water should not touch the bottom of the bowl.) Warm half the Drambuie in a small saucepan. Check the beef. If required rare, remove it from the oven and allow to rest, keeping it covered.

 2 minutes

Now add the warmed Drambuie to the yolks and keep whisking until they become a pale yellow colour. Remove from the heat, fold in the whipped double cream and taste the mixture; it should be light, fluffy and alcoholic! Remove the tomatoes from the oven.

4 minutes

If cooked, remove the swedes from the heat, drain and mash with the butter, season well and add grated nutmeg.

2 minutes

By now the potatoes should be cooked, if so remove, cool and drain. Mix the mayonnaise in a bowl with a little water so that it is thin and just coats the back of a wooden spoon. Add the chopped chives, slice the potatoes thinly and add to the mayonnaise.

2 minutes

Spoon some of the potatoes into the pastry cutter on a plate. Top this with the Arbroath smokie mixture and finally with the tomatoes. Remove cutter to reveal an impressive tower. Repeat for each serving. Serve with a little more of the sauce from the smokies.

2 minutes

Serve the beef on a bed of the swedes (neeps) with the sauce on top. Garnish with lightly steamed green vegetables or an asparagus stir fry, if desired.

 2 minutes

Serve the zabaglione in individual glasses with some of the reserved Drambuie and 5 crushed amaretti biscuits in the bottom of each glass.

2 minutes

CHICKEN LIVER AND SPECK SALAD

with

BLACK OLIVES AND SHERRY VINEGAR

CRISPY FRIED COD

with

MEDITERRANEAN VEGETABLES,

ROSEMARY MASH, AND

CITRUS DRESSING

IRISH COFFEE SOUFFLÉ

**Total cooking time for 3 courses
approximately 24 minutes and
preparation time 20 minutes**

Speck is cured and smoked belly of pork. It's not always easy to obtain, but it can easily be replaced with smoked bacon, whether streaky or back. Chicken livers seem to be much more in demand and so inexpensive these days, and fresh cod is also much less expensive than it used to be. Cooked in the way they are here, all these more traditionally plain flavours become quite deliciously different. You could also, if you wish, substitute the spicy tomato sauce used in menu 7 for the citrus dressing.

Don't be put off by the idea of a hot soufflé. It's actually very easy to do if you follow the instructions carefully. As we all know, the taste of Irish coffee is out of this world.

Left: Chicken Liver and Speck Salad with Black Olives and Sherry Vinegar

For the Chicken Liver Salad

INGREDIENTS

450 g/1 lb chicken livers (with sinew
    membranes removed)
170 g/6 oz speck (or smoked streaky bacon)
100 g/3½ oz black olives (unstoned, preferably)
1 head of frizée (or curly endive)
100 g/3½ oz baby spinach leaves
3 tbsp red wine
1 tbsp sherry vinegar
3 tbsp olive oil
Salt and freshly ground black pepper

EQUIPMENT

Frying pan
Chopping knife
Small bowl for the dressing
Pyrex bowl

PRE-PREPARATION

• If your butcher hasn't de-sinewed the livers you
may need to do this using a sharp knife.
• If you intend to keep the livers for a few days it
would be advisable to soak them in milk and store
them in the refrigerator. (The milk will preserve
them and at the same time remove any bitterness.)
• Heat the frying pan.
• Chop the bacon/speck into batons and season.
• Stone and cut the olives in half.
• Wash the salad leaves.

 5 minutes

For the Cod

INGREDIENTS

4 × 200 g/7 oz cod fillet steaks (with the skin on)
1 large courgette
1 aubergine
4 red peppers
1 yellow pepper
2 large potatoes
A little flour for dusting
Salt and freshly ground black pepper
Light olive oil
The juice of 1 orange
The juice of 1 lemon
The juice of 1 lime
1 dsp icing sugar
3 tbsp olive oil
3 tbsp double cream
1 large sprig of rosemary

EQUIPMENT

Frying pan
Griddle
Sharp knife
2 baking trays
Saucepan for boiling the potatoes
2 glass bowls
Small saucepan for hot dressing
Whisk
Potato masher

- Preheat the oven to (220°C/425°F, gas mark 7).
- Slice the courgette into lozenge shapes and the aubergine into rounds.
- Bake the peppers in the hot oven for 15 minutes until tender, proceeding with the other preparation in the meantime.
- Peel and cut the potatoes into 1-cm/½-inch cubes, cover with water and set to bring to the boil.
- Heat the frying pan and griddle.

10 minutes

For the Irish Coffee Soufflé

INGREDIENTS
85 g/3 oz unsalted butter
85 g/3 oz caster sugar
85 g/3 oz plain flour
3 egg yolks
8 egg whites
2 dsp instant coffee (blended with a little water)
1 tbsp Irish whiskey
55 g/2 oz soft butter
55 g/2 oz caster sugar
Icing sugar for dusting

EQUIPMENT
Small saucepan
Wooden spoon
Glass bowl for egg whites
Whisk
Pastry brush
4 × 10 cm/4-inch ramekins
Baking tray
Sieve

PRE-PREPARATION
- Preheat the oven to 200°C/400°F, gas mark 6. (If you are roasting the peppers, simply turn down the heat afterwards.)
- Melt the butter in a small saucepan, add the sugar and flour and blend in with a wooden spoon.
- Now add the egg yolks and blend in.
- Cook this mixture over a low heat until it leaves the side of the saucepan, removing from the heat after 4 minutes, allow to cool. (Start the main part of the cooking in the meantime.)

5 minutes

SEE OVER FOR METHOD

Firstly toss the fish fillets into seasoned flour, pat and dust off any excess.

½ *minute*

In the hot frying pan sear the fish in a little oil, skin side down, for approximately 1 minute.

1 *minute*

Turn the fish over, put on a baking tray and place in the preheated oven.

½ *minute*

Remove the peppers from the oven (after they have had 15 minutes), then either place in a bowl and cover with cling film to cool, or run under cold water, then remove the skins and seeds and reserve.

1 *minute*

Place the courgettes and aubergines in a bowl, cover with a little light olive oil and immediately remove and cook on the griddle pan for 2 minutes.

3 *minutes*

Pour a teaspoon of oil into the other frying pan and sear the speck and chicken livers for approximately 1 minute on each side, deglaze with the wine and remove from the heat. Check the fish and remove from oven if cooked; rerserve in a warm place.

2 *minutes*

Blend the sherry vinegar and olive oil together using a whisk and mix with the salad leaves.

1 *minute*

Warm the juices of the orange, lime and lemon in a saucepan. Whisk the icing sugar and olive oil together in a separate bowl, then add this to the warm citrus juices.

1 *minute*

Drain and mash the potatoes, add the cream and a little olive oil (1 dessert spoonful), season, add the rosemary leaves, and blend in well.

1 *minute*

Blend the livers, speck, leaves and dressing together to create a large ball of salad. Place the fish on top of the mashed potato, garnished with Mediterranean vegetables (peppers, aubergine and courgettes) and serve with citrus dressing.

3 *minutes*

About 14 minutes before you are ready to serve the pudding, whisk the egg whites in a clean bowl until they are at a ribbon stage (semi-peaks). Add the diluted coffee and Irish whiskey to the prepared base and blend in well. With a pastry brush, brush the butter around the soufflé dishes, dust with caster sugar, then carefully fold in the whisked egg whites into the base, blending well. Pour this mixture into the four soufflé dishes (ramekins), place on the baking tray and bake in the centre of the oven.

10 *minutes*

Remove, dust with icing sugar and serve immediately.

Right: Crispy Fried Cod with Mediterranean Vegetables, Rosemary Mash, and Citrus Dressing

MUSHROOM FEUILLÉTÉ

with

ASPARAGUS

TARTE TATIN OF PIMENTOS

PEACHES EN PAPILLOTE

with

BRANDY AND CREAM

**Total cooking time for 3 courses
approximately 27 minutes (18 minutes without the pudding)
and preparation time 21 minutes**

I haven't emphasised vegetarian dishes in particular, and many of the recipes in this book do use fish and shellfish rather than chicken or red meat. In fact, many of the starters throughout the book could be adapted to serve as vegetarian main courses. But this menu *is* entirely vegetarian!

Seasonal selections of mushrooms can be very wide, and here I've tried to make the most of them.

The pimento tarte tatin can become an everyday staple, and should please the palate of even a dedicated carnivore.

Don't be put off by what may look like a longer cooking and preparation time for these three courses; the steps are very simple.

For the Mushrooms

INGREDIENTS

350 g/12 oz shitake, oyster and button
    mushrooms
225 g/8 oz fresh asparagus
1 bunch of fresh tarragon (or 1dsp if dried)
225 g/8 oz puff pastry
1 egg yolk, beaten
A little cooking oil
25 ml/1 fl oz dry sherry or white wine
Salt and freshly ground black pepper
100 ml/4 fl oz double cream
Chervil to garnish

EQUIPMENT

Chopping knife
Rolling pin
10-cm/4-inch pastry cutter
Pastry brush
Saucepan for the asparagus
Baking tray

PRE-PREPARATION

• Preheat the oven to 230°C/450°F, gas mark 8 (this is for the peppers).
• Slice the mushrooms and trim the asparagus to lengths of approximately 7.5 cm/3 inches.
• Chop the tarragon.
• Roll out the pastry to a thickness of 3 mm/⅛ inch and cut into 4 10-cm/4-inch circles using the pastry cutter.
• Score the pastry in a criss-cross fashion and brush liberally with egg yolk.
• Bring a saucepan of salted water to the boil.

 6 minutes

Right: Tart Tatin of Pimentos

For the Tarte Tatin of Pimentos

INGREDIENTS

2 red peppers
2 green peppers
1 yellow pepper
2 medium courgettes
1 aubergine
2 large potatoes
Salt and freshly ground black pepper
A pinch of paprika
A little cooking oil
1 bunch of basil

EQUIPMENT

Baking tray
Knives
Grater
Frying pan (ovenproof)
Saucepan
Kitchen paper

PRE-PREPARATION

• Bring a saucepan of water to the boil (this is for the peaches).

• Place the peppers on a baking tray and roast in the oven preheated to 230°C/450°F, gas mark 8, for 15 minutes while you proceed with the rest of the preparation. Remove, put the peppers into a bowl and cover with cling film.

• Meanwhile, slice the courgettes into lozenges and the aubergine into rounds.

• Peel the potatoes and keep covered in cold water.

• Place a frying pan on a high heat.

11 minutes

For the Peaches

INGREDIENTS

4 large peaches
55 g/2 oz unsalted butter
55 g/2 oz caster sugar
100 ml/4 fl oz cooking brandy
Double cream to serve

EQUIPMENT

Saucepan
Knives
Aluminium foil
Greaseproof paper
Baking tray

PRE-PREPARATION

• Blanch the peaches for 10 seconds in boiling water, remove, refresh under cold running water and peel immediately.

• Slice the peaches away from the stone and then cut into thin slices.

• Make a parcel by laying together equal-sized squares of aluminium foil and greaseproof paper. When you are ready, the ingredients go on top of the paper to one side of the square, and the parcel is sealed by folding the other half over and crimping the edges around in a semi-circle like a cornish pastie. The foil helps hold the seal.

4 minutes

Place the pastry rounds on the baking tray and bake in a moderate oven at 200°C/400°F, gas mark 6, for approximately 7 minutes until brown and risen.

1 minute

Grate the potatoes on to a clean cloth, season with salt and squeeze out the juices. Now season with the paprika.

2 minutes

Fry the potato in a little oil in a hot frying pan until brown (usually 2 minutes), then turn over and repeat, then reserve.

2 minutes

Meanwhile, peel the peppers and cut into slices 2 cm/⅔ inch wide.

2 minutes

Remove the pastry from the oven. Blanch the asparagus in the boiling water for 2 minutes, adding the courgettes to the same water after 45 seconds. Remove and refresh.

2 minutes

Fry the aubergine slices in some oil in the hot frying pan until brown on both sides, remove and drain on kitchen paper. Wipe clean the frying pan with more kitchen paper.

2 minutes

Begin the tarte tatin by placing the peppers (alternately coloured) smooth side down into the frying pan. Top with the courgettes, some leaves of basil, seasoning and then finally the potato – filling the frying pan up. Place in the oven for 5 minutes.

3 minutes

Pour a little oil into the saucepan and heat, then sweat the mushrooms for 2 minutes. Deglaze with the sherry and season. Now add the cream and reduce to a consistency where it will coat the back of a spoon, add the tarragon and the asparagus.

3 minutes

Cut the pastry case in half and fill with the warm mushroom mixture. Place the lid on top and garnish with chervil and serve.

1 minute

Tip out the tarte tatin. The tart is excellent served with basil oil made from a bunch of basil blended with 150 ml/5 fl oz extra-virgin olive oil.

1 minute

Put the peaches, butter, sugar and brandy into the foil and paper parcel, fold over and crimp closed. Place on a baking tray and put into the oven for approximately 8 minutes at 200°C/400°F, gas mark 6.

Serve with double cream.

9 minutes

MENU 6

TUNA CARPACCIO

with

BLACK PEPPER AND LIME

———

BREAST OF DUCKLING

with

SAG ALOO AND

MARINATED CHERRIES

———

WHITE CHOCOLATE MOUSSE

with

STRAWBERRIES

**Total cooking time for 3 courses
approximately 16 minutes and
preparation time 27 minutes**

Carpaccio is usually served completely raw, but in this preparation of tuna we sear and salt it first. Although it can be prepared fairly quickly for best results you may want to plan ahead a bit. It may be raw in the middle, but the texture of the cooked, spicy outside makes this seem deliciously soft and silky rather than slippery. As soon as you realise how desirably subtle a flavour like this is, you're well on your way to becoming a true 'foodie'!

Duck is another distinctive taste, but one which most people already enjoy.

The white chocolate mousse is very simple to prepare, and doing it in advance means less hassle later on. It makes a clean, fresh finish to a rich and full-flavoured menu.

For the Tuna

INGREDIENTS

450 g/1 lb fresh tuna loin

A little olive oil

55 g/2 oz crushed black and white peppercorns
   (mignonette pepper)

The juice of 4 limes

25 g/1 oz icing sugar

100 ml/4 fl oz extra-virgin olive oil

A sprig of fresh tarragon (optional)

Salt and freshly ground black pepper

Salad leaves to garnish

EQUIPMENT

Frying pan

Cling film

Very sharp knife or meat slicer

Glass bowl for the dressing

Whisk

PRE-PREPARATION

• Heat the frying pan with a little olive oil until just smoking.

• Roll the tuna loin in the crushed peppercorns until coated and place in the hot pan, turning continuously to seal lightly all over.

• Tightly roll the tuna in cling film and place in the freezer (you should have cooked it so lightly that it is barely warm). Ideally leave until semi-frozen – approximately 2 hours – otherwise until needed.

6 minutes

For the Duckling

INGREDIENTS

4 Barbary duck breasts (225 g/8 oz each)

4 small potatoes

Salt and freshly ground black pepper

250 ml/8 fl oz dark chicken stock

175ml/6 fl oz red wine

900 g/2 lb fresh spinach

A little cooking oil

½ tsp ground nutmeg

1 tsp mild madras curry powder

250 g/8½ oz cherries, marinated in kirsch
   or brandy

EQUIPMENT

Knife

Small saucepan for the potatoes

Small saucepan for the chicken stock and sauce

Ovenproof frying pan

Small frying pan (or the tuna frying pan)

PRE-PREPARATION

• To prepare the Sag Aloo, peel the potatoes, cut into 1-cm/½-inch cubes, put in a saucepan of cold water (to cover) and season well. Cook until tender, approximately 10 minutes, while you proceed with the main part of the cooking.

• Meanwhile, combine the chicken stock and red wine and bring to the boil, then simmer until needed, by which time it should have reduced to a consistency where it will coat the back of a spoon.

• Wash and pick the stalks off the spinach.

• Preheat the oven to 220°C/425°F, gas mark 7.

6 minutes

For the Chocolate Mousse

INGREDIENTS

170 g/6 oz white chocolate

2 leaves of gelatine

150 ml/5 fl oz double cream, semi-whipped

225 g/8 oz strawberries (or available soft fruit)

1 tsp icing sugar

EQUIPMENT

Saucepan and a glass bowl that will fit over the
    top (bain marie)

450-g/1-lb terrine mould or loaf tin

Cling film

Sharp knife

PRE-PREPARATION

• Bring some water to the boil in a saucepan, place
a bowl over the top (the water shouldn't touch the
bottom of the bowl) and melt the chocolate. Allow
the gelatine to moisten in approximately 1 tablespoon of warm water. Squeeze the gelatine to
extract the water, add this to the chocolate, and stir
well in. Fold in the semi-whipped double cream.

• Line the terrine mould with cling film.

• Slice the strawberries and dust with the icing
sugar.

• Pour the chocolate into the mould until it is half
filled, then add the sliced strawberries, reserving a
few slices for garnish.

• Pour over the remaining chocolate and allow to
set for 2–3 hours in the fridge.

15 minutes

SEE OVER FOR METHOD

Heat the ovenproof frying pan and add a little oil. Season the duck breasts well and fry in the pan skin side down, then turn over and seal the other side. Place in the preheated oven for 8–10 minutes.

2 *minutes*

Remove the tuna from the freezer (if it is frozen solid allow to thaw for ½ hour beforehand) and slice it thinly through the cling film – carefully remove the cling film afterwards.

2 *minutes*

Mix the lime juice with the icing sugar and olive oil and whisk well. Chop the tarragon and season.

1 *minute*

Dress the leaves in a little of the above dressing and arrange in the centre of the plates.

2 *minutes*

Now neatly arrange the thin slices of tuna around each salad garnish. Add the tarragon to the remaining dressing and pour over the tuna slices. This is now ready to serve.

2 *minutes*

Remove the duck from the oven and allow to rest for two minutes. Meanwhile, heat some oil in a frying pan and fry the cooked potato until lightly browned, then add the nutmeg and curry powder.

2 *minutes*

Now add the spinach to the pan and allow it to wilt. Taste and check the seasoning.

½ *minute*

Taste the chicken stock and wine sauce and add the cherries with some of their liquor. If the sauce is too thin you can whisk in 55 g/2 oz of unsalted butter (optional).

1 *minute*

Serve the Sag Aloo (spinach and potato) in the centre of the plate. Slice the duck and spread it over the top. Serve the sauce over it with plenty of cherries.

2 *minutes*

Unmould the white chocolate mousse, slice and garnish with a few of the sliced strawberries.

1 *minute*

CRISPY FRIED RED SNAPPER

with

SPICY SALSA

POT ROASTED

BREAST OF GUINEA FOWL

with

GARLIC RÖSTI AND GINGER STIR FRY

CRÊPES SUZETTE

with

SAMBUCCA

**Total cooking time for 3 courses
approximately 21 minutes and
preparation time 27 minutes**

Red snapper is fairly widely available, although if you have problems finding it, the salsa works equally well with red mullet.

Guinea fowl makes a change from chicken, and a rösti like this is especially good with garlic.

Crêpes Suzette are an old dinner party favourite, which like all good things have come back to our tables again. It's one of the most delicious puddings ever.

For the Snapper

INGREDIENTS

4 small red snapper fillets (115 g/4 oz each),
   with their skins
1 red pepper
1 green pepper
2 red chillies
2 green chillies
A little seasoned flour
Salt and freshly ground black pepper
1 tbsp white wine vinegar
3 tbsp white wine
3 tbsp extra-virgin olive oil
A few mixed leaves (e.g. baby lettuce, lamb's
   lettuce, rocket)
Chervil to garnish (optional)
A little cooking oil

EQUIPMENT

Chopping knife
Frying pan
Palette knife
Kitchen paper
Saucepan

PRE-PREPARATION

• Preheat the oven to 200°C/400°F, gas mark 6.
• Cut the peppers in half, remove the seeds, slice
into julienne strips, then finely dice these strips.
• Cut the chillies in half, remove the seeds, and
finely chop.

4 minutes

For the Guinea Fowl

INGREDIENTS

2 whole guinea fowl (preferably corn-fed)
2 large potatoes
4 garlic cloves
A 5-cm/2-inch square of fresh root ginger
Cooking oil
The juice of 2 limes
¼ bottle of red cooking wine
1 sprig of fresh thyme or 1 tsp dried thyme
   (optional)
Salt and freshly ground black pepper
100 g/3½ oz baby sweet corn
100 g/3½ oz mangetout
100 g/3½ oz baby spinach

EQUIPMENT

Knives
Grater
Tea-towel
Garlic crusher
Ovenproof frying pan
Aluminium foil or greaseproof paper
Non-stick frying pan
Wok
Skewer

PRE-PREPARATION

• Bone the guinea fowl to remove the breasts and
legs from the carcass, or ask your butch to do this.
• Peel and grate the potato into the clean tea-
towel. Crush the garlic and add to the potato.
• Peel and shred the ginger.

8 minutes

For the Crêpes Suzette

INGREDIENTS

for the pancake batter
2 eggs
A pinch of caster sugar
250 ml/8 fl oz milk for the pancake batter
100 g/3½ oz plain flour
A dash of olive oil

A little vegetable oil
55 g/2 oz unsalted butter
115 g/4 oz caster sugar
The juice and zest of 2 oranges
50 ml/2 fl oz Sambucca or Pernod

EQUIPMENT

Glass bowls for the batter
Whisk
Sieve
Frying pan or pancake pan
Ladle
A small saucepan

PRE-PREPARATION

• Prepare the pancake batter by blending the ingredients with a whisk in a glass bowl and then passing the batter through a sieve into a clean bowl.
• Heat a frying pan until hot, then pour in a little vegetable oil and swirl it around the pan. Tip this off, then add a ladleful of the pancake batter and swirl it so it covers the base of the pan.
• Cook each pancake until it browns, then turn it over and brown the other side.

15 minutes

Left: Crêpes Suzette with Sambucca

Season the guinea fowl, then sear the birds in the ovenproof frying pan in a little cooking oil until lightly coloured on both sides.

2 minutes

Now pour in the lime juice and red wine, and add the thyme. Cover with foil (or greaseproof paper) and cook in the preheated oven for 8–10 minutes.

1 minute

Whilst the guinea fowl are cooking, dust the red snapper fillets with a little seasoned flour and heat a small frying pan.

1 minute

Fry the fish fillets for 1 minute, skin side down, in the pan until crisp, then turn over and seal the other side for 30 seconds, no more. Remove and drain on kitchen paper.

1½ minutes

Mix the vinegar, white wine and olive oil together in a small saucepan, add the chopped peppers and the chillies and warm through gently.

1 minute

Place a frying pan on a high heat and add a little oil. Season the grated potatoes and crushed garlic with salt (still in the cloth) and squeeze out the juices to obtain dry grated potato.

1 minute

In the hot frying pan fry the potato until brown.

1 minute

CONTINUED

Now flip the potato over, turn down the heat and cook the other side for approximately 5 minutes.

1 minute

Meanwhile, heat the wok, pour in a little oil, and add the ginger. When the ginger starts to cook, add the sweet corn and fry until brown. Add the mangetout and the spinach and, if necessary, a little water. Season well.

2 minutes

Remove a guinea fowl from the oven and check that it is cooked by inserting skewer into the centre. Remove the skewer and rest it on your lips – if it is hot the guinea fowl is cooked, if it is warm or cool, leave the guinea fowl in the oven for a few more minutes.

2 minutes

Place the butter and the sugar for the pudding in a saucepan. When the butter starts to melt add the orange juice and the zest and cook until the sauce amalgamates to a consistency where it will coat the back of a spoon. Remove the potato from the heat.

2 minutes

Fold the pancakes into quarters, place in the sauce and poach for a few minutes.

1 minute

Start to serve up by arranging some of the mixed leaves in the centre of one plate. Dress them with a little of the warm chilli salsa, reserving some for the snapper. Warm up the snapper for 1 minute in a hot oven.

1 minute

Pour some of the salsa sauce around the red mullet, garnish with chervil and serve.

½ minute

Serve the rösti in the centre of the plate and garnish it with some of the stir fry, pouring the sauce from the roasting pan around (but taste and season it if necessary first).

1 minute

When ready to serve the pancakes, remove them from the sauce and place on individual plates. Pour the Sambucca into the sauce and ignite (carefully), using either the gas flame or a match, to burn off the alcohol. Pour over the pancakes.

2 minutes

KING PRAWNS

with

CHILLIES AND PORCINE LINGUINE

HONEY ROASTED BREAST OF DUCK

with

ORIENTAL STIR FRY

TROPICAL FRUITS

with

ORANGE LIQUEUR

**Total cooking time for 3 courses
approximately 13 minutes and
preparation time 17 minutes**

There's more oriental influence at work here in the king prawns served with chillies, and the spicy duck dish that follows too. The pasta served with the prawns doesn't have to be the porcine mushroom one I've specified; even if you don't make your own, you can buy perfectly good fresh pasta from most supermarkets. King prawns in their shells can be pricey, but because they're so much bigger, you'll use fewer than you would with the fiddlier, smaller ones.

Right: King Prawns with Chillies and Porcine Linguine

For the Prawns

INGREDIENTS

12 large Pacific prawns or Mediterranean prawns
   (in their shells)
2 green chillies
1 red chilli
2 shallots
2 garlic cloves
150 g/5½ oz Porcine (cep) Linguine
100 ml/4 fl oz olive oil
50 ml Sushi vinegar (or white wine vinegar)
A pinch of caster sugar
Vegetable oil for frying
Juice of 1 lemon
1 tsp sea salt
Small bunch fresh coriander leaves
25 g/1 oz butter
Salt and freshly ground black pepper

EQUIPMENT

Chopping knife
Sieve (or colander)
Frying pan
Saucepan for pasta
Pasta fork or metal fork

PRE-PREPARATION

• Cut chillies in half, remove and discard the seeds, and chop finely. Finely chop the shallots, and crush the garlic with the flat of a knife blade and chop.

• Blanch the pasta for approximately 4 minutes in boiling salted water with a teaspoon of olive oil. (Proceed with the duck preparation in the meantime.) Drain, refresh immediately under cold running water and set aside.

 6 minutes

For the Duck

INGREDIENTS

4 Barbary duck breasts, medium weight
    (approx. 200 g/7 oz)
1 heaped tbsp clear honey
1 tsp paprika
1 tbsp olive oil
1 packet mangetout (approx. 150 g/5½ oz)
1 packet baby sweet corn (approx. 150 g/5½ oz)
1 packet shitake mushrooms (approx. 150 g/5½ oz)
150 ml/5 fl oz light soy sauce
Juice and zest of 2 lemons
1 bunch fresh coriander
Salt and freshly ground black pepper
A little vegetable oil or sesame oil

EQUIPMENT

Small saucepan
Sharp knife
Frying pan
Baking tray
Wok
Plastic spatula

PRE-PREPARATION

• Melt the honey, paprika and olive oil together in a
small saucepan and set aside.
• Shred the mangetout and slice the sweet corn in
half lengthways, slice the mushrooms.
• Preheat a frying pan and the oven to
230°C/450°F, gas mark 8.
• Chop the coriander leaves.

4 *minutes*

For the Tropical Fruits

INGREDIENTS

1 mango
1 pawpaw
8 lychees
1 watermelon
100 ml/4 fl oz Cointreau or other orange liqueur
Juice of 1 lemon
2 passion fruits
150 g/5½ oz fromage frais (sweetened with a
    little icing sugar if the liqueur is less sweet)
Cocoa, to dust

EQUIPMENT

Peeler (ideally a 'French', T-shaped one) and
    sharp knives
Glass bowl
Suitable glasses
Fine sieve, for dusting

PRE-PREPARATION

• Peel the mango to remove the skin and then slice
the flesh into neat pieces.
• Peel the pawpaw, cut it in half, remove the seeds,
and cut into neat slices.
• Peel and remove the stones of the lychees.
• Remove the watermelon rind and cut the flesh
into neat cubes.
• Marinate all of the fruit in the liqueur with the
lemon juice for as long as you are able.

7 *minutes*

SEE OVER FOR METHOD

Rub the melted honey mixture into the skins of the duck breasts and fry (skin side down) in a little oil to brown and crisp the skin. Place on a baking tray and roast in the preheated oven for 8 minutes. Place a wok to heat up on the burner used for frying the duck.

2 minutes

Sweat the garlic, shallots and chillies in a little olive oil in the hot frying pan, add the prawns, vinegar and sugar.

1 minute

Now add the remainder of the olive oil, and the lemon juice and sea salt. Allow to simmer over a low heat for 3 minutes.

1 minute

Start the stir fry in the hot wok by sweating the sweet corn in a little oil with the mushrooms, using the spatula. Add the soy sauce, lemon juice and zest, and turn down the heat to a very low simmer.

2 minutes

Add the chopped coriander to the prawns, remove them from the heat and let rest. Meanwhile, reheat the pasta in the butter in a saucepan for 2 minutes on a low heat.

2 minutes

Cut the passion fruits in half and remove the seeds with a spoon and stir into the fruit and Cointreau mixture.

1 minute

Season the pasta, remove from the pan and make a tower, using the pasta fork to twirl the noodles, in the centre of a plate. Serve the prawns around.

1 minute

Remove the duck breasts from the oven (keep warm if not serving immediately), slice each breast into 3 or 4 pieces and serve with the stir-fried vegetables.

2 minutes

Before serving, put the fruits and juices into the individual glasses, top with fromage frais and dust with cocoa.

1 minute

Left: Honey Roasted Breast of Duck with Oriental Stir Fry

PESTO PASTA

with

WILD MUSHROOMS

―――

MILLEFEUILLE OF ASPARAGUS

with

CARAMELISED ONIONS AND TABBOULEH

―――

POACHED PEACHES

FLAMBÉ

**Total cooking time for 3 courses
approximately 24 minutes and
preparation time 30 minutes**

Tabbouleh is bulgar wheat and, like couscous, takes on other flavours very well, such as the garlic and lemon juice here. These two savoury dishes should put paid to any meateater's notion that vegetarian food is bland. The millefeuille uses a filo pastry for crisp contrast to the soft onions and asparagus.

End all this with peaches flamed in brandy and you'll be host of the year!

For the Pasta

INGREDIENTS

150 g/5½ oz fresh tomato (or spinach)
    pasta tagliatelli
Olive oil
Salt and white pepper
2 garlic cloves
A bunch of fresh coriander
1 large bunch of basil
2 tbsp freshly grated Parmesan
Juice of 1 lemon
150 g/5½ oz assorted field mushrooms
1 tbsp sweet sherry

EQUIPMENT

Saucepan for the pasta
Garlic crusher
Knives
Food processor
Frying pan
Small saucepan for reheating the pasta

PRE-PREPARATION

• Bring a saucepan of water to the boil and add a
tablespoon of olive oil and salt. Blanch the fresh
pasta for approximately 2 minutes (until the water
comes back to the boil) then immediately refresh
under cold running water.
• Meanwhile, peel and crush the garlic.
• Chop the coriander.

3 *minutes*

For the Millefeuille

INGREDIENTS

150 g/5½ oz filo pastry
1 large bunch asparagus (approximately
    450 g/1 lb)
1 egg, beaten
1 garlic clove
1 large onion
1 bunch of fresh parsley
1 tbsp fresh tarragon or 1 tsp dried
Olive oil
A little cooking oil
1 tsp sugar
100 g/3½ oz tabbouleh (cracked wheat)
Salt and freshly ground black pepper
The juice of 1 lemon

for the sauce
150 ml/5 fl oz double cream
3 tbsp dry white wine

EQUIPMENT

Pastry brush
Pastry cutter 9–10 cm/3½–4 inches in diameter
Sharp knife
Saucepan for the asparagus
Baking tray
Frying pan
Saucepan for the tabbouleh
Saucepan for the sauce

For the Peaches

PRE-PREPARATION

• Preheat the oven to 200°C/400°F, gas mark 6.
• Cut the asparagus into 10-cm/4-inch pieces and blanch in a saucepan of boiling salted water with a little olive oil for 2 minutes. Refresh immediately under cold running water.
• Spread out 2 sheets of filo pastry and brush each one with the egg. Place the sheets on top of each other and cut out 3 discs per portion (12 in all) using your pastry cutter.
• Peel, chop and paste the garlic clove. Peel and slice the onion.
• Chop the parsley.
• Chop the tarragon (unless using dried).
• Heat a frying pan. Boil some water to cover the tabbouleh.

12 minutes

INGREDIENTS

4 large peaches
280 ml/9 fl oz sugar syrup (see page 87)
3 tbsp cooking brandy
Pouring double cream to serve

EQUIPMENT

Saucepan
Serving bowls
Ladle

PRE-PREPARATION

• Prepare the sugar syrup according to the instructions on page 87.
• Poach the peaches (in their skins) in the sugar syrup at a low simmer for approximately 10 minutes until the peaches are soft and tender. Remove the peaches, reserving the syrup.
• When cool (run under a cold tap, or set aside in a bowl covered with cling film), remove the skins of the peaches and replace in the poaching liquor.

15 minutes

SEE OVER FOR METHOD

Put the basil, Parmesan and garlic in a food processor with a tablespoon of olive oil and lemon juice and blend until it becomes a smooth paste. Taste and season with salt and a little white pepper.

3 *minutes*

Place the pastry filo discs on a baking tray and bake in the preheated oven for approximately 3 minutes (as for the tuna recipe, page 13).

1 *minute*

Meanwhile, pour a little oil into the hot frying pan and sweat the sliced onion with the sugar until it starts to caramelise (if necessary, add a little liquid – either some white wine or just a little water).

2 *minutes*

Place the tabbouleh in a small saucepan, cover with boiling water, add the garlic and the lemon juice and simmer on a low heat until the tabbouleh is tender (about 2 minutes).
   Take the pastry discs out of the oven and remove them from the tray.

1 *minute*

In a hot pan, sweat the mushrooms in a little olive oil, then add the sherry, season, add the coriander, and stir well.

2 *minutes*

Remove the tabbouleh from the heat and stir in the parsley. In a small saucepan with a little olive oil start warming the pre-cooked pasta, then add the pesto mix and stir well in.

2 *minutes*

Serve a tower of the pesto pasta in the centre of the plate with a few mushrooms around the tower.

2 *minutes*

Meanwhile, add the blanched asparagus to the now cooked onions, with little wine if necessary, reheat thoroughly (2 minutes or so) and season.

2 *minutes*

Reduce down the cream for the sauce for 2 minutes, then add the wine, reduce again for 1 minute, and add the tarragon.

3 *minutes*

Start constructing the layers of the millefeuille by first putting a filo disc on the plate. Spread with some tabbouleh, then the onions and asparagus mixture, and repeat so that you have two layers and finish with a layer of filo pastry on top. Serve a little of the sauce around.

3 *minutes*

Remove the poached peaches from the syrup and place in a bowl. Add half the brandy to the sugar syrup and bring to the boil. Pour the remaining brandy into a ladle and ignite, either from the gas flame or using a match.

3 *minutes*

Pour the flaming brandy over the peaches and serve with double cream on the side.

1 *minute*

SALMON PAPILLOTE

with

LIME LEAVES

SPRING CHICKEN

with

WASABI AND GARLIC,
MUSHROOM RISOTTO

CAMBRIDGE PUDDING

**Total cooking time for 3 courses
approximately 20 minutes and
preparation time 13 minutes**

Cooking something *en papillote* means steaming it within a paper, but in practice it can also mean an aluminium foil parcel. The advantage of this method is that it retains all the flavour of the ingredients, and they all inherit the flavours of each other.

Arborio rice is the most popular for risotto, but another short-grain rice will also work well.

Cambridge pudding is a local speciality at my restaurants. If you don't have a microwave, the traditional method is easily mastered, and the pudding will be ready when you have eaten the other two courses. But the microwave version takes only a minute – do try it!

Right: Salmon Papillote with Lime Leaves

For the Salmon

INGREDIENTS

340 g/12 oz salmon (cut into 4 × 85-g/3-oz
    boneless steaks or escalopes)
1 tbsp white wine (per parcel)
1 tbsp olive oil (per parcel)
The juice of 2 limes
Salt and freshly ground black pepper
2 kaffir lime leaves

EQUIPMENT

Aluminium foil
Greaseproof paper
A large baking tray (or 2 medium-sized trays)
Serving plates

PRE-PREPARATION

• Fold the foil, lined with greaseproof paper, into 1
or 2 pockets in which to cook the fish (depending
on the size of the steaks).

2 minutes

For the Chicken

INGREDIENTS

4 spring chickens, medium weight (150 g/6 oz)
1 tsp Wasabi mustard powder
1 dsp honey
2 garlic cloves, peeled and crushed
200 ml/7 fl oz vegetable stock
2 shallots
A little cooking oil
350 g/12 oz assorted mushrooms, shitake,
    oyster, etc.
200 g/7 oz Arborio (risotto) rice
3 tbsp double cream

EQUIPMENT

Garlic crusher (or back of a large knife)
Small saucepan for the vegetable stock
Frying pan
Saucepan
Baking or roasting tray
Wooden spoon

PRE-PREPARATION

- Preheat the oven to 220°C/425°F, gas mark 7.
- Mix the wasabi, honey and crushed garlic together with a little water to form a loose, spreadable paste.
- Rub or brush this paste into the breast of the chickens.
- Put the chickens into the roasting tray and leave to roast in the oven for 20 minutes (approximately, depending on the size of the chicken) while you proceed with the other steps.
- Prepare the vegetable stock (see page 8) and set to bring to the boil.
- Finely chop the shallots and chop the mushrooms into approximately 3 pieces.
- Heat the frying pan and saucepan.

10 *minutes*

For the Cambridge Pudding

INGREDIENTS

175 g/6½ oz mixed dried fruit
Sufficient cooking brandy to cover dried fruit
1 egg
175 g/6½ oz plain flour
1 tsp baking powder
100 g/3½ oz soft butter, plus a little extra
    for the ramekins
100 ml/4 fl oz milk
1 tsp mixed spice
½ tsp cinnamon
115 g/4 oz granulated sugar
A little clotted cream for garnish

EQUIPMENT

Glass bowl for preparing the mixture
Ramekin dishes or similar microwave-proof
    dishes
Pastry brush for buttering the ramekins

PRE-PREPARATION

- Cover the dried fruit with the brandy and leave to marinate for as long as you are able.
- Lightly butter the ramekins.
- The 'quick' version used in this recipe is especially adapted for microwave use. If you don't have a microwave, change the milk quantity to 300 ml/16 fl oz, and add 175 g/6½ oz soft cake crumbs. Follow the same method steps, but steam in a large pan, each ramekin covered with pleated foil, for 40–45 minutes while you cook the other two courses.

1½ *minutes (for microwave method)*

SEE OVER FOR METHOD

Pour a little oil into the large saucepan, sweat the shallot until just tender, but not coloured, add the rice, stir in with a wooden spoon, and then add 2–3 ladlesful of hot vegetable stock.

1 minute

Pour a little oil into the hot frying pan and sweat the mushrooms until tender, 2 minutes. Now add these to the rice with another ladleful of vegetable stock, if necessary. (Stir now and again as you proceed.)

3 minutes

Meanwhile, place the salmon inside the parcels and 1 tbsp white wine and 1 tbsp olive oil per parcel, and the juice of the limes. Season the salmon, add the lime leaves to the parcel and fold up. Bake the fish in the hot oven for approximately 5 minutes until the parcels puff up and the outside crimps of the greaseproof paper brown, but the salmon remains pink inside.

1 minute

Add the egg, flour, baking powder, butter, milk, mixed spice and sugar to the dried fruit mixture and blend together with a wooden spoon until smooth.

2 minutes

Pour this mixture into the lightly buttered ramekins, filling the dishes half full.

1 minute

Check the risotto and, if necessary, add more stock. Taste and check for seasoning, then add the cream and stir well to produce a smooth risotto.

1 minute

Remove the fish from the oven and allow to rest. At the same time, check whether the chicken is cooked by inserting a small knife or needle into the thighs; the juices should run clear. If not, keep in the oven a little longer.

2 minutes

Start to remove the chicken from the bone, place on a baking tray and put back in the oven if the chicken is slightly underdone.

2 minutes

Serve the salmon on small plates. Serve the risotto on a plate with the chicken on top.

2 minutes

When ready, put the ramekins in the microwave, 2 at a time for 1–1½ minutes on full power for a 750-watt oven, or adjust accordingly.

2 minutes

Check the puddings are firm. If still wet and runny put back in the microwave for a further 15 seconds.

½ minute

Allow puddings to rest for 1 minute, then unmould the puddings and serve with the clotted cream on top.

2 minutes

Left: Spring Chicken with Wasabi and Garlic, Mushroom Risotto

MENU II

CROSTINI OF CHICKEN LIVERS

with

PAK CHOI AND CHILLI

———

MARINATED CHUMP OF LAMB

with

BLACK OLIVES,

PROVENÇAL HERBS AND

TURMERIC MASH

———

AMARETTI TRIFLE

**Total cooking time for 3 courses
approximately 18 minutes and
preparation time 28 minutes**

Crostini, small pieces of fried bread cooked with lots of garlic, make an excellent crisp base to any first course, such as these chicken livers. The Chinese leaves, pak choi, and the chillies add a little oriental influence. If you're not a chicken liver fan, then use pigeon breast instead, as we do in the restaurant, or even simple slivers of chicken breast, which will still retain the style of the dish.

Chump of lamb means the cut from the hind quarter, effectively the rump. It's a bit more fatty than the lean and tender loin section, but it marinades and will griddle and roast better. In the oven, the fatty juices run out, leaving a tasty, tender piece of meat. Just leave any extra fat at the side of your plate!

For the Crostini

INGREDIENTS

450 g/1 lb chicken livers
1 French stick
2 garlic cloves
Salt
1 light pak choi lettuce (see notes on vegetables)
Vegetable oil
2 red chillies
3 tbsp soy sauce

EQUIPMENT

Sharp knife
Garlic crusher
Frying pan or wok
Saucepan
Kitchen paper

PRE-PREPARATION

• De-sinew the livers (or ask your butcher to), remove the cores from the centre, and wash away any blood under cold water.
• Cut the bread into 4 neat lozenge shapes, approximately 2 cm/1 inch thick.
• Peel the garlic, crush, then spread on to the bread shapes.
• Bring a saucepan of salted water to the boil.
• Wash and chop the pak choi.
• Halve the chillies, remove seeds, then chop finely.
• Preheat a frying pan.

8 *minutes*

For the Lamb

INGREDIENTS

4 × 200 g/7 oz chump steaks of lamb
   (or leg of lamb steaks)
200 ml/7 fl oz lamb stock
3 medium-sized potatoes
85 g/3 oz unsalted butter
1 tbsp olive oil
Salt and freshly ground black pepper
1 dsp turmeric (or saffron)
3 tbsp medium sherry
3 dsp black olives, pitted

for the marinade
100 ml/4 fl oz olive oil
1 large sprig of rosemary
3 garlic cloves, crushed
1 tbsp Herbes de Provence (dried)
Salt and freshly ground black pepper

EQUIPMENT

Dish for marinating the lamb
Saucepan for the sauce
Peeler
Griddle
Baking tray
Potato masher

SEE OVER FOR PRE-PREPARATION

Right: Crostini of Chicken Livers with Pak Choi and Chilli

- Preheat the oven to 200°C/400°F, gas mark 6.
- Mix the marinade ingredients together and marinate the lamb for as long as you can.
- Reduce the stock in the saucepan by half its volume; it should coat the back of a spoon.
- Peel and boil the potatoes until tender as you prepare the other courses.
- Heat a griddle.

5 minutes

For the Trifle

INGREDIENTS

For the crème pâtissière

3 egg yolks
45 g/1½ oz caster sugar
200 ml/7 fl oz milk
55 g/2 oz plain flour, sifted
100 ml/4 fl oz double cream
55 g/2 oz icing sugar to sweeten double cream, to taste

250 g/8½ oz Italian amaretti biscuits
200 g/7 oz cherries, marinated in kirsch (or brandy)
115 g/4 oz dark chocolate, grated
A few sprigs of fresh mint

EQUIPMENT

Bowls
Whisk
Saucepan
Sieve

PRE-PREPARATION

Make 200 ml/7 fl oz crème pâtissière as follows:

- Whisk the sugar and the yolks until creamy.
- Bring the milk to the boil.
- Add the flour to the egg and sugar and stir in.
- Pour on the milk and whisk until you have a thick custard. Pass through a sieve and allow it to cool.
- Semi whip the double cream to ribbons, with the icing sugar, if desired.

15 minutes

Sear the lamb on both sides on the hot griddle, then put on the baking tray and roast in the preheated oven for 10–12 minutes.

2 *minutes*

Fry the lozenges of bread in a little vegetable oil until golden on each side, then drain on kitchen paper.

2 *minutes*

Pour a little vegetable oil into the hot frying pan or wok and sweat the chicken livers for approximately 1½ minutes each side. Set aside to rest.

3 *minutes*

Meanwhile, blanch the chopped pak choi in the saucepan of boiling water for 30 seconds, then remove and refresh under cold running water.

1 *minute*

Mash the potato with the butter and olive oil and season generously. Add the turmeric or saffron and blend in well.

2 *minutes*

In the crostini frying pan, fry the pak choi in a little vegetable oil with the chilli and add the soy sauce.

1 *minute*

Serve the chicken livers on a little of the pak choi on each crostini with some of the soy juices around. Remove the lamb from the oven and allow to rest in a warm place.

1 *minute*

Add the sherry to the sauce and bring back to the boil, add the olives, taste and season.

Crush the amaretti biscuits and put equal quantities into the glasses. Soak these with a heaped tablespoon of the marinated cherries and then a little crème pâtissière.

3 *minutes*

Top this with more of the cherries and some of the sweetened double cream. Garnish with some grated chocolate and a sprig of mint.

1 *minute*

Thinly slice the lamb and arrange over a neat portion of turmeric potato. Serve the sauce around the lamb.

1 *minute*

BRUSCHETTA

with

GRILLED VEGETABLES

———

POACHED BREAST OF CHICKEN

with

A BROTH OF VEGETABLES AND HERBS

———

BITTER CHOCOLATE

CRÈME BRÛLÉE

**Total cooking time for 2 courses
approximately 19 minutes and
preparation time for 3 courses 31 minutes**

Bruschetta is taken from the Italian word *bruscare*, meaning to roast over coals. A traditional garlic bread, drenched in olive oil and baked in the oven, when topped with tomatoes, aubergines, peppers or any other Mediterranean vegetable, becomes an exciting starter. The mâche, or lamb's lettuce, is widely available pre-packed in supermarkets, but use what you can find.

The poached breast of chicken is deliciously light and herby, which the chocolate crème brûlée sets off rather wickedly.

For the Bruschetta

INGREDIENTS

1 French stick
1 red pepper
3 plum tomatoes
2 garlic cloves
Balsamic vinegar
Olive oil
Salt and freshly ground black pepper
Curly endive and lamb's lettuce to garnish
1 aubergine
The juice of 1 lemon
1 tsp Herbes de Provence
Sprigs of fresh basil

EQUIPMENT

Sharp knife
Garlic crusher
Bowl to dress the leaves
Baking tray

PRE-PREPARATION

• Slice the pepper into strips (approximately
2×4 cm/¾×1½ inches) and remove the seeds.
• Slice the tomatoes into even-sized 1-cm/½-inch
pieces.
• Peel and crush the garlic.
• Mix together a 50–50 blend of balsamic vinegar
and olive oil (to make approximately 3 tablespoons)
and season.
• Wash the salad leaves. Preheat the grill.

6 minutes

For the Chicken

INGREDIENTS

4 chicken breasts, skinned and boneless
   (approx. 175 g/6 oz each)
150 ml/5 fl oz chicken stock
2 shallots
1 garlic clove
A selection of baby vegetables
300 ml/10 fl oz vegetable stock
Chopped chives to garnish
A little vegetable oil
100 ml/4 fl oz dry white wine
1 egg yolk
1 lemon
1 sprig of rosemary
1 egg yolk

EQUIPMENT

Sharp knife
Small saucepan for the vegetables
Large saucepan for the chicken
Stainless steel bowl
Whisk
Saucepan

PRE-PREPARATION

• Prepare the chicken stock (see page 8; you can
use either fresh or a cube).
• Precook the baby vegetables in the vegetable stock
(see page 8 – either fresh or a cube) until tender, then
refresh immediately under cold running water.
• Peel and finely chop the shallots.
• Peel and finely chop the garlic.
• Chop the chives.

10 minutes

For the Brûlée

INGREDIENTS

250 g/8½ oz dark bitter chocolate
600 ml/21 fl oz double cream
5 egg yolks
55 g/2 oz icing sugar, plus extra for dusting

EQUIPMENT

Saucepan large enough to accommodate the
    stainless steel bowl
Stainless steel bowl
Saucepan
Bowl for egg yolks and sugar
Whisk
Ramekins
Baking dish to hold the ramekins in the oven
Wooden spoon
Ladle
Aluminium foil

PRE-PREPARATION

• Preheat the oven to 150°C/300°F, gas mark 2.
• Bring a saucepan of water to a simmer, place a stainless steel bowl over the saucepan (ensuring that the water doesn't touch the sides) and melt the chocolate.
• Warm the cream in a saucepan. Whisk together the egg yolks and sugar.
• Have the ramekins ready in a baking dish half filled with warm water (hot tap temperature).
• Pour the cream into egg yolk and sugar mixture, stir in the chocolate, and blend.
• Ladle this mixture into the ramekins, leaving approximately 1 cm/½ inch space at the top of each ramekin. Cover the baking dish with foil but pierce it to allow the steam to escape.

 15 minutes

SEE OVER FOR METHOD

Place the brûlées in the preheated oven, or 25 minutes before you want to serve them. Cut the French stick at an angle into slices approximately 1.5 cm/⅔ inch thick, spread a little garlic on each and soak with olive oil.

2 *minutes*

Place on a baking tray and bake in the oven for approximately 10 minutes. Meanwhile, cut the aubergine into slices ½ cm/¼ inch thick, place on a baking tray with the tomatoes and pepper, dribble with olive oil and lemon juice, sprinkle with the dried herbs and grill for 2–3 minutes.

4 *minutes*

Fry the shallots and garlic in a little oil until translucent in a large saucepan. Add the white wine and boil for 1 minute. Remove the vegetables from the grill.

3 *minutes*

Add the chicken breasts and rosemary to the wine sauce and seal each side. Add the chicken stock and poach the chicken for 10–15 minutes.

1 *minute*

Meanwhile, in a stainless steel bowl, whisk the egg yolk with a little drop of boiling water and, over a saucepan of boiling water continue whisking until creamy and thick. Remove from the heat.

2 *minutes*

Remove the bruschetta from the oven and build each one with a piece of aubergine, some tomato and pepper, season with salt, and garnish with sprig of basil.

3 *minutes*

Dress the leaves with the balsamic dressing and lemon juice and arrange the leaves in the centre of each serving plate. Place one bruschetta in the middle of the leaves and serve.

2 *minutes*

Add the egg mixture to the chicken when it is cooked, along with the cooked vegetables, and stir well in. Taste and adjust seasoning.

1 *minute*

Now add the chopped chives and stir in. Serve the chicken in the centre of a shallow bowl (or soup plate) with the broth around.

1 *minute*

Check the brûlées in the oven – look for the 'wobble factor', by which I mean the mix should wobble slightly but not be loose enough to spill should you jolt the dish. If not cooked, allow another 5–10 minutes and check regularly. When ready, remove and allow the brûlées to rest and cool down.

To serve, dust liberally with icing sugar and glaze under the grill or use a blow torch.

SLIVERS OF SALMON

with

CHABLIS

GRIDDLED CALVES' LIVER

with

PANCETTA AND ONION JUICES

PEAR TARTE TATIN

**Total cooking time for 3 courses
approximately 18 minutes and
preparation time 25 minutes**

It's a myth that there's any danger in eating fresh raw fish. It's been a staple in Japan for centuries, and the Japanese have enviable health and longevity records. But this salmon isn't totally raw in any case. The Chablis marinade goes to work on it, and you could always add a dash of lemon juice, lime juice or vinegar to act as an acid, which will also act as a 'cooking' agent.

Calves' liver is one of my wife Sally's favourite foods, cooked medium to well done. For this dish, slice the liver thinly and cook it quickly if you want it left pink in the middle. Pancetta is an Italian bacon that is cured in salt and spices.

Pear tarte tatin is another family favourite. It's simple but positively brilliant.

For the Salmon

INGREDIENTS
350 g/12 oz salmon fillet
100 ml/4 fl oz chablis (or other dry white wine)
100 ml/4 fl oz olive oil
Juice of 1 lemon
1 small bunch spring onions
A selection of various leaves for garnish
   (e.g. baby lettuce, lamb's lettuce, rocket)
3 tbsp balsamic vinegar
3 tbsp olive oil
Salt and freshly ground black pepper

EQUIPMENT
Knives
Dish for marinating the salmon
Bowl for dressing the leaves
Serving plate

PRE-PREPARATION
• Thinly slice the raw salmon into small but long slithers.
• Prepare the marinade by mixing together the wine, 100 ml/4 fl oz olive oil and lemon juice and place the salmon in it as you proceed with the other preparation.
• Wash and finely chop the green parts of the spring onions. Wash the salad leaves.

5 minutes

For the Calves' Liver

INGREDIENTS
675 g/1½ lb calves' liver (skinned and prepared)
Olive oil
2 large potatoes
150 ml/5 fl oz vegetable stock
1 tsp yeast extract
100 ml/4 fl oz red wine
2 garlic cloves
115 g/4 oz pancetta
1 large and 2 small onions
Salt and freshly ground black pepper

EQUIPMENT
Sharp knife
Peeler
Saucepan for the potatoes
Saucepan for the sauce
Garlic crusher
Griddle or frying pan
Potato masher
Wooden spoon

SEE OVER FOR PRE-PREPARATION

• Ensure the liver has had the thin membrane (or skin) removed. If you are buying a whole piece of liver you will need to thinly slice it and cover it with olive oil to prevent it drying up (allow 2 slices per portion, approximately 170 g/6 oz).

• Peel and chop the potatoes into 2.5-cm/1-inch pieces, place in a saucepan, cover with water, add salt, bring to the boil and cook until tender as you prepare the rest of the meal.

• Place the vegetable stock, yeast extract and red wine together in a small pan and place over a medium heat to reduce to a coating consistency (about half the original volume).

• Peel and slice the onions thinly and add to the simmering sauce to cook until tender.

• Peel, crush and paste the garlic.

10 minutes

For the Pear Tarte Tatin

INGREDIENTS

5 large firm pears
225 g/8 oz puff pastry
100 g/3½ oz unsalted butter
100 g/3½ oz caster sugar
1 egg, beaten
Clotted cream to serve

for the sugar syrup
250 ml/8 fl oz water
175 g/6½ oz caster sugar
1 stick of cinnamon

EQUIPMENT

Peeler
Sharp knife
Rolling pin
Non-stick frying pan
Saucepan
Pastry brush

PRE-PREPARATION

• Peel and core the pears and slice in half.

• Roll out the pastry to fit over the frying pan (a little larger to allow for shrinkage).

• Prick the pastry to prevent it rising.

• Bring the syrup ingredients to the boil, add the pears and poach gently until tender (approximately 10 minutes) while you proceed with the main part of the cooking.

• Preheat the oven to 200°C/400°F, gas mark 6.

10 minutes

Left: Griddled Calves' Liver with Pancetta and Onion Juices

SEE OVER FOR METHOD

Heat the griddle ready to cook the calves liver.

½ *minute*

Melt the butter and sugar in the frying pan ready for the pears.

2 *minutes*

After 2 minutes, put in the poached pears (rounded side down) and caramelise (colour) for a minute or so.

2 *minutes*

Now place the pastry on top, brush with the beaten egg and place in the preheated oven for approximately 15 minutes until golden brown.

1 *minute*

Remove the calves' livers from the olive oil, season and place on the hot griddle for 30 seconds each side.

1 *minute*

Allow the liver to rest. Meanwhile, dress the leaves for the salmon by blending the vinegar and remaining olive oil together with a little seasoning, and toss well together.

1 *minute*

Arrange the slices of salmon neatly around the plate and dress the centre with a tall pile of the leaves using a pastry cutter as a mould, if desired, to aid the shape and height.

2 *minutes*

Taste the salmon marinade and, if necessary, add a little more wine or seasoning, then add the chopped spring onions and use to dress each plate. Serve.

1 *minute*

Mash the cooked potatoes and add about 1 tablespoon olive oil with the crushed and pasted garlic. Mix well, then return the saucepan to the heat. Keep stirring well with a wooden spoon. Check the wine sauce for consistency.

2 *minutes*

Griddle or grill the pancetta for approximately 10 seconds and remove. Quickly reheat the liver on the griddle or in the oven and remove after 30 seconds.

3 *minutes*

Pour the sauce over the calves' liver and garnish it with the pancetta on top. Serve.

1 *minute*

Remove the tartew tatin from the oven and serve with a dollop of clotted cream on each plate.

1 *minute*

MOULES MARINIÈRE

with

SMOKED BACON AND CHIVES

BREAST OF CHICKEN

with

BUBBLE AND SQUEAK

AND LEMON SAUCE

APPLE FRITTERS

with

TOFFEE SAUCE

**Total cooking time for 3 courses
approximately 19 minutes and
preparation time 23 minutes**

Moules marinière is another all-time favourite. But adding smoked bacon gives it an unusual twist, although obviously you can omit this to keep the dish suitable for vegetarians. Serve your moules piled high in bowls for maximum impact.

The bubble and squeak recipe is very similar to my rösti, but with the addition of cabbage and onion.

Enjoy the toffee apple fritters as a warming winter finale.

Left: Moules Marinière with Smoked Bacon and Chives

For the Moules Marinière

INGREDIENTS

1 kg/2.2 lb fresh farmed mussels
3 garlic cloves
2 shallots
8 rashers of smoked lean back bacon
1 large bunch of fresh chives
Salt and freshly ground black pepper
375 ml/13 fl oz dry white wine
150 ml/5 fl oz water
115 g/4 oz unsalted butter (chilled)

EQUIPMENT

Sharp knife
Deep saucepan with a fitted lid

PRE-PREPARATION

• Scrub the mussels, remove the beards and any barnacles.
• Crush the garlic with the flat of a knife and chop, and finely chop the shallots.
• Chop the bacon into small batons.
• Finely chop the chives.

10 minutes

For the Chicken

INGREDIENTS

4 chicken breasts, skinned and off the bone
   (175 g/6 oz each)
2 large potatoes
1 onion
1 cabbage
100 ml/4 fl oz chicken stock (a cube, if necessary)
100 ml/4 fl oz red wine
Cooking oil
The juice of 2 lemons
Salt and freshly ground black pepper

EQUIPMENT

Peeler
Grater
Sharp knife
Saucepan for the sauce
Frying pan
Roasting or baking tray

PRE-PREPARATION

• Mix the chicken stock with the red wine and reduce in a saucepan to a consistency where it coats the back of a spoon. This takes about 10 minutes, and will be ready when you are ready to use it.

• Peel and grate the potatoes.

• Peel and finely slice the onion.

• Finely chop the cabbage.

• Preheat the oven to 200°C/400°F, gas mark 6.

• Preheat the frying pan.

8 minutes

For the Apple Fritters

INGREDIENTS

4 English eating apples

140 g/5 oz cornflour ⎫
140 g/5 oz plain flour ⎭ sifted together

Water to blend to a smooth paste

250 ml/8 fl oz vegetable oil

55 g/2 oz sesame seeds

for the toffee sauce

55 g/2 oz unsalted butter

115 g/4 oz soft brown sugar

150 ml/5 fl oz double cream

EQUIPMENT

Sharp knife

Bowl for mixing the batter

Deep frying pan

Slotted spoon

Kitchen paper

2 saucepans for the toffee sauce

Sieve

PRE-PREPARATION

• Peel and core the apples and cut each into 5 × 2.5 cm/ 1 inch pieces.

• Sift the flours together and mix with the water until it forms a smooth but thick batter.

• Heat the oil in a deep frying pan until it reaches a temperature of 170°C/335°F.

5 minutes

SEE OVER FOR METHOD

Pour a little oil into the preheated frying pan and sear the chicken breasts on both sides.

1 *minute*

Place on a roasting tray in the preheated oven, and roast for 8 minutes.

Mix the potato with the cabbage and the onion, put into the frying pan with a little oil and cook on a medium heat until lightly browned, then flip over and cook the other side. Reserve in a warm place.

3 *minutes*

Meanwhile, sweat the shallots and the garlic in a deep saucepan with the bacon, then add the mussels and stir well. Add the white wine and water, and simmer until all the shells have opened up.

1 *minute*

Dip the apples into the batter and deep fry in the hot oil until golden brown. Remove with a slotted spoon and drain on kitchen paper.

3 *minutes*

Melt the butter, add the soft brown sugar, stir to blend and cook for approximately 2 minutes.

2 *minutes*

Remove the chicken from the oven and allow to rest.

1 *minute*

Now add the double cream to the sugar/butter mixture, stir in and pass through a sieve into a clean saucepan. Reserve.

1 *minute*

Add the lemon juice to the reduced chicken stock and taste for seasoning.

1 *minute*

Add the butter to the mussels and season well. Add the chives and stir together well. Serve the mussels and some of the juices in a deep bowl or soup plate.

2 *minutes*

Slice the chicken breasts in half and serve on top of a slice of the bubble and squeak. Serve with the lemon sauce (and perhaps some roasted vegetables – see menu 1).

1 *minute*

Serve the fritters (warmed through in the oven for 2–3 minutes) with the toffee sauce poured over them, and sprinkled with sesame seeds.

3 *minutes*

Left: Breast of Chicken with Bubble and Squeak and Lemon Sauce

GRILLED SQUID TERIYAKI

PAN-FRIED SEA BASS

with

TARRAGON PESTO AND

DAUPHINOISE POTATOES

CHOCOLATE KAHLUA

POTS

**Total cooking time for 3 courses
approximately 17 minutes and
preparation time 28 minutes**

I don't know about you, but I adore squid. It cooks quickly, isn't chewy like octopus, and served teriyaki-style with all those wonderful oriental soy, ginger, spring onion and garlic flavours, your taste buds can hardly do it justice. This is the sort of food I love: explosive in flavour, exciting to look at, creative and simple.

I have kept the pretty fishy theme with a delicious tranche of sea bass, which has got to be Britain's premium fish. The pesto dressing won't overpower it, and means you don't risk smothering it with a sauce.

No apologies for the chocolate pudding: I love chocolate too, and this is a quick, simple way of ending another wonderfully balanced menu.

For the Squid

INGREDIENTS

450 g/1 lb baby squid (washed and cleaned)
1 bunch of spring onions
1 garlic clove
1 lime
2 red chillies
100 ml/4 fl oz soy sauce
1 tsp ground ginger (or 2 cm/¾-inch piece
   fresh root ginger, grated)
1 tbsp sake or white or rice wine vinegar
1 dsp honey
Fresh coriander
The juice of 2 lemons
Olive oil, freshly ground black pepper
250 g/8½ oz rocket leaves

EQUIPMENT

Sharp knife
Garlic crusher
Small saucepan
Baking tray

PRE-PREPARATION

• To make the Teriyaki, finely chop the spring
onions, peel and crush the garlic, squeeze the lime
and de-seed and chop the chillies. Mix all of these
ingredients with the soy sauce, ground ginger, sake
and honey, put into a saucepan and warm gently.
• Chop the squid into small rings (ensure that they
have been washed and cleaned before doing this),
leaving the tentacles whole. Place on a baking tray.
• Chop the coriander.
• Preheat the grill on a high heat.

8 *minutes*

For the Sea Bass

INGREDIENTS

4 × 200 g/7 oz sea bass fillets

for the pesto
A little plain flour
Salt and freshly ground black pepper
1 large bunch fresh tarragon
100 g/3½ oz fresh Parmesan
Juice of 1 lemon
115 ml/4½ fl oz olive oil
2 garlic cloves
2 tbsp pine kernels

for the dauphinoise potatoes
3 garlic cloves
3 large baking potatoes
150 ml/5 fl oz double cream
55 g/2 oz cheddar cheese

EQUIPMENT

Food processor
Non-stick frying pan
Kitchen paper
Garlic crusher
Mandolin or sharp knife
Saucepan

• Preheat the oven to 200°C/400°F, gas mark 6.
• Prepare the pesto by blending the tarragon leaves (approximately a wine glassful) with the Parmesan and lemon juice and a little (1 tablespoon) olive oil and the garlic.
• Pan fry the pine kernels in a little oil to colour and brown, drain on kitchen paper.
• Add the pine kernels to the tarragon mixture and blend in a food processor for one minute.
• Crush the garlic ready for the potatoes and peel the potatoes.

10 *minutes*

For the Chocolate Pots

285 g/10 oz bitter dark chocolate
300 ml/10 fl oz double cream
2 egg yolks
55 g/2 oz caster sugar
100 ml/4 fl oz Kahlua or Tia Maria

Saucepan and stainless steel bowl (bain marie)
Bowls
Whisk
Ramekin dishes

• Bring a saucepan of water to a simmer, place a stainless steel bowl on top (ensuring that the water doesn't touch the sides of the bowl) and melt the chocolate.
• Semi-whip the cream so that it forms ribbons.
• Whisk the eggs and sugar together until creamy (2 minutes).
• Add the cream and eggs to the chocolate with all but 3 tablespoons of the Kahlua and pour into ramekins. Allow to chill while you cook and serve the rest of the meal.

10 *minutes*

SEE OVER FOR METHOD

Slice the potatoes very thinly, using a mandolin or knife. Bring the cream to the boil with the garlic, add the potatoes and cook for 15 minutes.

3 *minutes*

Heat a little oil in the frying pan used for the pine kernels. Coat the sea bass with seasoned flour, dusting off any excess.

2 *minutes*

Fry the fish skin side down until it is crispy (1 minute), then turn over and seal the other side. Remove the fish from the pan. Bake in the oven for 7–10 minutes.

2 *minutes*

Pour the lemon juice over the squid, cover with olive oil and season with black pepper, then grill for 3–5 minutes.

3 *minutes*

Check the potatoes for tenderness and stir gently.

1 *minute*

Remove the squid from the grill. Dress the rocket leaves with some of the teriyaki dressing and serve the squid around the leaves with plenty of the teriyaki juices.

2 *minutes*

Mix the tarragon pesto with approximately 100 ml/4 fl oz olive oil to make a dressing. Taste and season as necessary.

1 *minute*

The fish and potatoes should be ready at the same time. Remove the fish from the oven and serve on a bed of the cooked dauphinoise potatoes with the pesto dressing around each portion. Accompany it with a green vegetable or green salad (such as rocket and Parmesan, if desired).

2 *minutes*

Before serving, remove the chocolate pots from the fridge, they should be firm and smooth, but not hard. Pour at least another 3 tablespoons of Kahlua over each pot.

1 *minute*

MENU 16

POACHED SALMON,
NAGE JUICES AND DEEP-FRIED LEEKS

with

WILD RICE

VENISON STEAK

with

GARLIC AND ROSEMARY AND
CHIANTI SAUCE

CARAMELISED BANANA,
CHANTILLY CREAM AND RUM

**Total cooking time for 3 courses
approximately 21 minutes and
preparation time 20 minutes**

The word *nage* derives from the French verb *nager,* to swim. And this is actually the effect we want to achieve. You should be able to see little pieces of salmon swimming in the juices around the wild rice topped with crispy fried leeks.

Venison is one of the leanest and most tasty meats available. Ensure you obtain venison steaks or saddle of venison for the utmost tenderness; cuts from the haunch need marinating for a while in advance.

Right: Poached Salmon, Nage Juices and Deep-fried Leeks with Wild Rice

For the Salmon

INGREDIENTS

350 g/12 oz fresh salmon
200 ml/7 fl oz nage (vegetable stock),
   see page 8
1 vegetable stock cube dissolved in 150 ml/5 fl oz
   water
1 large leek
200 ml/7 fl oz deep frying oil
100 g/3½ oz wild rice
2 tbsp flour
Salt and freshly ground black pepper
55 g/2 oz unsalted butter (chilled)
The juice of 1 lemon
Small bunch fresh basil (or 1 tbsp dried)
Small bunch fresh coriander (or 1 tbsp dried)
Small bunch fresh parsley or chives
   (or 1 tbsp dried)

EQUIPMENT

Sharp knife
Saucepan for deep frying
Saucepan for the rice
Kitchen paper
Slotted spoon
Deep saucepan for poaching the salmon
Whisk
Sieve

PRE-PREPARATION

• Mix the vegetable stock cube with 150 ml/5 fl oz
water and bring to the boil.
• Skin, bone and cut the salmon into 4 steaks and
place in a saucepan.
• Prepare the nage (see page 8).
• Cut the leek into julienne strips.

10 minutes

For the Venison

INGREDIENTS

4 × 170–200 g/6–7 oz venison saddle steaks

2 garlic cloves

1 large sprig of fresh rosemary (or 2 tsp dried)

Salt and freshly ground black pepper

Light olive oil

1 dark chicken stock cube and vegetarian stock
   cube or 150 ml/5 fl oz game stock

375 ml/13 fl oz Chianti or other red wine

2 large sweet potatoes

55 g/2 oz butter

Vegetables of your choice, optional

EQUIPMENT

Garlic crusher

Dish or bowl for marinating the venison

Saucepan

Baking tray

Large frying pan

PRE-PREPARATION

• Put the sweet potatoes on to a baking tray and
bake for 40–45 minutes in an oven preheated to
220°C/425°F, gas mark 7 as you cook the rest of the
meal, and serve the starter.

• Peel and crush the garlic and put it in a dish with
the rosemary and the venison steaks, season and
cover with olive oil. (The marinade gives the venison
added flavours, it is not needed to tenderise the
meat as the saddle is a very tender, lean cut.)

• Dissolve the stock cubes in 150 ml/5 fl oz water
and start to reduce with the red wine. (Alternatively,
you can use 150 m/5 fl oz game stock.)

7 *minutes*

For the Bananas

INGREDIENTS

5–6 bananas

55 g/2 oz unsalted butter

100 g/3½ oz soft brown sugar

1 dsp ground cinnamon

1 tsp ground nutmeg

100 ml/4 fl oz double cream

55 g/2 oz icing sugar

1 vanilla pod (optional)

3 tbsp rum

EQUIPMENT

Wooden spoon

Glass bowl for the butter and sugar mixture

Baking tray

Glass bowl for the cream

Sieve

Whisk

PRE-PREPARATION

• Mix the butter in the bowl until soft, then add the
brown sugar and spices.

• Preheat the grill (or hot oven).

3 *minutes*

SEE OVER FOR METHOD

Heat the oil for deep frying and cover the wild rice with the vegetable stock and bring back to the boil, simmer for 15 minutes.

1 minute

Toss the julienne strips of leek in the flour and season with a little salt. Dust off the excess flour and have some kitchen paper ready for draining.

1 minute

When the oil starts bubbling and reaches approximately 170°C/335°F, deep fry the leeks for 10–15 seconds, remove immediately with a slotted spoon and drain.

½ minute

Bring the nage to the boil and as soon as it boils turn it down to a simmer. Meanwhile heat the frying pan ready for the venison.

1 minute

Seal the venison on both sides in a little of the marinade and put on an ovenproof tray and roast with a little of the garlic and rosemary from the marinade for 7 minutes. (If the sweet potatoes are nearly cooked, the oven temperature can be reduced to 200°C/400°F, gas mark 6.)

2 minutes

Peel the bananas and coat with the sugar and butter mixture.

2 minutes

Poach the salmon in the nage juices for 4 minutes in a saucepan covered with a lid or piece of greaseproof paper.

1 minute

Meanwhile, start chopping the herbs ready to finish the salmon sauce.

2 minutes

Now start grilling the bananas, 2 minutes each side. Whilst they are cooking, remove the salmon, whisk the chilled butter into the nage with the lemon juice, add the herbs, and taste and season.

Take the venison out the oven and allow to rest.

4 minutes

Remove the bananas and whip the cream, sifted icing sugar and the seeds from the vanilla pod.

2 minutes

Rinse the wild rice with boiling water in the sieve, then serve the salmon on top of a little wild rice with plenty of the sauce around and garnished with the crispy leeks.

2 minutes

Take the cooked sweet potatoes and cut them in half. Remove the potato flesh, mash with a little butter, season well, and either pipe or spoon back into the potato skins.

Slice the venison thickly into 3–4 pieces per portion, at an angle for tender eating, and serve it with the sweet potato (and, optional, other vegetables) and sauce the dish.

2 minutes

Pour the rum over the warm bananas and serve with some of the Chantilly cream on the side.

1 minute

Right: Venison Steak with Garlic and Rosemary

MENU 17

CEVICHE OF SALMON

with

MUSTARD SEED DRESSING

———

GRIDDLED CHUMP OF LAMB,
AUBERGINE CONFIT AND RED CABBAGE

———

AMERICAN PANCAKES

with

ICE CREAM AND

CANADIAN MAPLE SYRUP

**Total cooking time for 3 courses
approximately 30 minutes and
preparation time 25 minutes**

Ceviche of salmon is often seen as a restaurant dish, but as another one of those cooked/uncooked fish starters it's indispensable for a quick menu like this, and should also become more widely known at home anyway. The salmon gets marinated in small cubes with shallots and capers, citrus juice and fresh herbs, and in just a short time the fish is infused and tastes out of this world. Neatly presented as a gâteau, and topped with some tart fromage frais, it's the sort of starter that provides maximum impact and flavour with the minimum of effort.

The chump of lamb here comes with hearty red cabbage and an aubergine confit. This very quick way of cooking aubergine is adapted from the Gascon method of preserving meat by cooking it in fat to seal it and pack in flavours. Here the flavouring agent is the garlic.

Classic American pancakes are very simple and quick. I did them on-air for ITV's *Afternoon Live*, and the response from viewers for the recipe was enormous. Be sure to drench them in the maple syrup.

For the Ceviche

INGREDIENTS

350 g/12 oz Salmon

for the dressing
100 ml/4 fl oz olive oil
1 tsp English mustard
2 dsp yellow mustard seeds
Juice of 1 orange
1 tsp icing sugar

1 tbsp capers
The juice of 2 limes or lemons
2 shallots
A bunch of fresh coriander (or basil)
Salt and white pepper
150 g/5½ oz fromage frais
Chervil to garnish

EQUIPMENT
Bowls for the dressing and the salmon
Sharp knife
Large pastry cutter
Palette knife
Whisk

PRE-PREPARATION

• Prepare the dressing by whisking together all the ingredients in a bowl.

• Cut the salmon into 1 cm/½ inch pieces, put in a bowl, add the capers and cover with the lime (or lemon) juice. Season.

• Chop the shallots and coriander, add to the salmon, season and stir well. Marinate the salmon for at least ½ hour as you prepare the rest of the meal to allow all the flavours to infuse.

10 minutes

For the Lamb

INGREDIENTS

4 × 225 g/8 oz lamb chump steaks
1 medium red cabbage
100 ml/4 fl oz white wine vinegar
350 ml/12 fl oz red wine
250 g/8½ oz soft brown sugar
200 g/8 oz redcurrant jelly
Salt and freshly ground black pepper
100 g/3½ oz sultanas
250 ml/8 fl oz lamb stock
1 large aubergine
250 ml/8 fl oz cooking oil
2 garlic cloves

EQUIPMENT
Sharp knife
Baking dish or roasting tray for the cabbage
Aluminium foil
Griddle
Saucepan for the sauce
Saucepan for the aubergine
Roasting tray

SEE OVER FOR PRE-PREPARATION

Right: Griddled Chump of Lamb, Aubergine Confit and Red Cabbage

For the Pancakes

PRE-PREPARATION

• Finely shred the red cabbage, place in a large saucepan, stir in the vinegar, 200 ml/7 fl oz of the red wine and the sugar, and jelly.

• Add the sultanas, stir in, cover and boil for 15–20 minutes until tender, as you cook the rest of the meal.

• Mix the stock and the remaining red wine together in a saucepan and start to reduce. By the time you will need it, it should be half its volume, and coating the back of a spoon.

• Preheat the griddle.

• Cut the aubergine into 10×6 cm/4×2½ inch pieces. Preheat the cooking oil with the 2 whole (peeled) cloves of garlic.

 10 minutes

INGREDIENTS

115 g/4 oz plain flour

A pinch of caster sugar

2 tsp baking powder

175 ml/6 fl oz milk

1 egg

4 portions of vanilla ice cream

150 ml/5 fl oz Canadian maple syrup

EQUIPMENT

Mixing bowls

Whisk

Sieve

Pancake or frying pan

Ladle

Large pastry cutter, approximately
    15 cm/6 inches in diameter

Ice cream scoop

PRE-PREPARATION

• Mix the flour, sugar, baking powder and milk and egg together until it becomes a smooth batter, then pass through a sieve into a clean bowl.

• Preheat the pancake pan.

 5 minutes

SEE OVER FOR METHOD

Griddle the lamb steaks for 1–2 minutes, turn over and seal the other side.

3 *minutes*

On a roasting tray roast the lamb in the oven for 15–20 minutes.

½ *minute*

Put the aubergine into the warm oil with the two cloves of garlic, cook until golden brown (usually 5 minutes or so), then turn over.

2 *minutes*

Press out the juices from the salmon using a spoon and pack a quarter of it into the pastry cutter (which should be slightly greased inside) allowing a gap at the top of ½ cm/¼ inch for the fromage frais. Put on to the first course plates, leaving the ring in place, and top with the fromage frais. Repeat until you have 4 neat rings of ceviche.

8 *minutes*

Remove the aubergine confit from the saucepan, drain on kitchen paper and keep warm.

½ *minute*

Add a little oil to the preheated pancake pan and heat until it smokes, then tip off any excess.

1 *minute*

Ladle the pancake batter into the pan into a large pastry cutter ring, to a thickness of about 1 cm/½, cook until golden brown, approximately 2 minutes. Flip it over and cook the other side for 1–2 minutes, remove from the pan and repeat, 1 pancake per portion, as you complete the rest of the meal.

4 *minutes*

If you like your lamb pink, remove it from the oven and allow it to rest. (If you would like the lamb cooked more, leave it in the oven for a further 5 minutes or so.)

2 *minutes*

Check the sauce (it should coat the back of a spoon) and, if necessary, add more red wine. Taste and season. Remove the red cabbage from the oven, stir well, and check to see that it is tender.

2 *minutes*

Whisk the dressing ingredients together again for the salmon and spoon a little around each ceviche. Garnish the salmon with a little chervil. Serve.

2 *minutes*

Thinly slice the lamb and arrange on a small pile of the red cabbage in the centre of each main course plate. Garnish with the aubergine confit and pour over the sauce.

4 *minutes*

Serve a scoop of vanilla ice cream on each pancake and drizzle liberally with maple syrup.

1 *minute*

MENU 18

TIAN OF CRAB MEAT

with

PICKLED CUCUMBER, SHERRY VINEGAR

FILLET OF BEEF

with

WHISKY, NEEP AND TATTIE CAKES

DRAMBUIE SYLLABUB

with

CRÈME FRAÎCHE AND CHERRIES

**Total cooking time for 3 courses
approximately 30 minutes and
preparation time up to 28 minutes**

Left: Tian of Crab Meat with Pickled Cucumber, Sherry Vinegar

This menu is in many ways a variation of menu 7, and is mainly Scottish. While Scotch beef is undoubtedly the best, the crab can come from elsewhere — Cornwall, for instance.

I'd like to claim the neep-and-tattie cakes as my own invention, even if they too are a variation on a traditional theme. Their creaminess combines with the tender cuts of beef and rich red wine sauce absolutely mouthwateringly.

Finish off with a light and frothy syllabub, lightened with crème fraîche and fresh cherries — but I wouldn't blame you for making it as alcoholic as possible!

For the Crab

INGREDIENTS

1 large fresh, cooked, cock crab, weighing
 1.1–1.35 kg/2½–3 lb
 (or 3 × 200 g/7 oz cans crab meat)
1 cucumber
3 tbsp white wine vinegar
1 dsp caster sugar
Salt and freshly ground black pepper
Small bunch fresh coriander (or 1 tbsp dried)
1 tsp ground ginger
55 g/2 oz unsalted butter (melted)

for the dressing
3 tbsp sherry vinegar
3 tbsp extra virgin olive oil
Salt and freshly ground black pepper

EQUIPMENT

Peeler
Mandolin or sharp knife for slicing the cucumber
Bowl or dish for pickling the cucumber
Sharp knife
Glass bowl for mixing the crab meat
Ring or pastry cutter, approximately
 7.5 cm/3 inch in diameter
Bowl for the dressing
Whisk

PRE-PREPARATION

• Peel and thinly slice the cucumber. Mix together the wine vinegar and sugar, and season. Add the cucumber into this pickle and allow it to absorb the flavour. (It will keep well, but does start to become wet and slushy after a few days.)

• If using fresh crab, first remove all the white meat and then the brown meat from the head. (Discard the spongy gills – known as 'dead man's fingers'.)

• Chop the coriander.

10 minutes (if using fresh crab)

For the Beef

INGREDIENTS

4 × 200 g/7 oz fillet steaks (trimmed weight)
450 g/1 lb baking potatoes
450 g/1 lb swede
Salt and freshly ground black pepper
170 g/6 oz seasoned soft breadcrumbs
Vegetable oil
85 g/3 oz unsalted butter (softened)
A little grated nutmeg

for the sauce
150 ml/5 fl oz vegetable stock
100 ml/4 fl oz red cooking wine
½ tsp yeast extract
1 tbsp whisky

EQUIPMENT

Peeler
Sharp knife
Saucepans for the potatoes and the sauce
Frying pan for the beef and the potato cakes
2 baking trays
Potato masher

PRE-PREPARATION

• Preheat the oven to 200°C/425°F, gas mark 7.
• Peel and chop the potato and swede into small
1-cm/½-inch dice, place in a saucepan, cover with
cold water, season well with salt and bring to the
boil as you proceed with the rest of the meal. When
tender, drain well and reserve for mashing.
• Heat all the sauce ingredients except for the
whisky and start reducing the liquid.
• Preheat a frying pan for the steaks.

 10 minutes

For the Syllabub

INGREDIENTS

225 g/8 oz fresh cherries
75 ml/3 fl oz Drambuie
55 g/2 oz icing sugar
250 g/8½ oz crème fraîche/Mascarpone
Tuile pastry biscuits (optional)

EQUIPMENT

Bowl for marinating the cherries
Bowl for the crème fraîche mixture
Wooden spoon
Suitable glasses

PRE-PREPARATION

• Stone, then marinate the cherries in the Drambuie
while you prepare the rest of the meal.
• Blend the icing sugar and the crème fraîche or
Mascarpone together.

 8 minutes

SEE OVER FOR METHOD

Left: Fillet of Beef with Whisky, Neep and Tattie Cakes

Pour a little oil into the preheated frying pan and sear the beef fillets on both sides, then place them on a baking tray and put into the oven for 5–7 minutes.

3 *minutes*

Mash the potato and swede together and season if necessary. Add a tablespoon of the breadcrumbs to the mixture to make it drier, then add the butter and nutmeg and work in.

2 *minutes*

Mould the potato mix into 7.5-cm/3-inch cakes, then drop into the remaining breadcrumbs and coat thoroughly.

3 *minutes*

Check the beef (it will need 5 minutes for rare, 7–10 minutes for medium rare), and, when ready, remove and allow it to rest.

1 *minute*

Start mixing the crab, ginger and butter together, season, and add the coriander.

2 *minutes*

Fry the potato cakes in a little vegetable oil until golden brown, then place on a baking tray and finish in the oven for 5 minutes. If the beef is cooked, the temperature can be reduced to 200°C/400°F, gas mark 6.

5 *minutes*

Check the sauce for seasoning, and for consistency; it should be able to coat the back of a spoon.

½ *minute*

Mould the crab into the pastry ring, first putting a ring of cucumber on the bottom and then 1 cm/½ inch of crab meat. Add another layer of cucumber and then another 1 cm/½ inch of crab meat. Finish with a final ring of cucumber (see photograph). Mould straight on to the plates. Remove the potato cakes from the oven.

8 *minutes*

Blend the olive oil and sherry vinegar together, taste and season. Use to dress the crab.

2 *minutes*

Serve the beef with a potato cake. Finish the sauce by adding the whisky; allow the alcohol to burn off for a minute or two, and then pour over the beef.

2 *minutes*

Serve the marinated cherries at the bottom of the glasses and pour over the crème fraîche mixture. If available, garnish with tuile pastry biscuits.

2 *minutes*

ROSEMARY ROASTED MONKFISH

with

NOODLES

ENTRECÔTE OF BEEF

with

SATAY DIP AND TINY FRIES

PINEAPPLE COLADA

**Total cooking time for 3 courses
approximately 34 minutes and
preparation time 18 minutes**

The main course here is, in effect, a version of good old steak and chips. But these chips are a bit different: cut very finely, they can be cooked in the frying pan with just a little bit of oil — there's no need for deep frying.

The rich, nutty satay sauce adds a new slant to the dish, and off-sets the simpler monkfish starter.

A creamy pineapple colada is a very good palate-cleanser, and very refreshing.

For the Monkfish

INGREDIENTS

350 g/12 oz monkfish tail, trimmed and skinned
Olive oil
A sprig of fresh rosemary for the fish
   (or 1 tsp dried)
Salt and freshly ground black pepper
2 dsp white wine
1 dsp white wine vinegar
A sprig of fresh rosemary for the sauce
115 g/4 oz unsalted butter (chilled)
Juice of ½ lemon
150 g/5½ oz Chinese egg noodles
A small sprig of fresh rosemary to garnish

EQUIPMENT

Sharp knife
Bowl
Cling film
Saucepan for the noodles
Saucepan for the sauce
Ovenproof roasting dish/tray
Whisk
Sieve or colander

PRE-PREPARATION

• Reduce the white wine and vinegar together with the rosemary to make a syrup.
• Meanwhile, cut the monkfish into 4 equal-sized pieces to speed up the cooking process and place in a bowl.
• Cover the fish with olive oil, sprinkle with rosemary and season well. Cover with cling film and keep in the fridge until needed.
• Bring a saucepan of salted water to the boil for the noodles.
• Preheat the oven to 200°C/400°F, gas mark 6.

6 minutes

For the Entrecôte

INGREDIENTS

4 × 225 g/8 oz entrecôte (sirloin steaks)
125 g/4½ oz unsalted peanuts
2 garlic cloves
25 g/1 oz brown sugar
1 tsp chilli powder (or 2 fresh chillies, de-seeded)
1 tsp ground coriander seeds
½ tsp cumin
1 medium onion
3 large potatoes (Maris Piper or similar)
250 ml/8 fl oz vegetable oil
100 ml/4 fl oz coconut milk (or double cream)
200 ml/7 fl oz vegetable stock
1 tbsp soy sauce
The juice of 1 lemon
Salt and freshly ground black pepper

EQUIPMENT

Food processor
Peeler
Sharp knife
Deep fat fryer
Saucepan
Roasting tray
Slotted spoon
Kitchen paper

PRE-PREPARATION

• For the satay grind the peanuts with the garlic, sugar, chilli, spices and onion in a food processor.
• Peel the potatoes and finely chop into small fries (approximately 4 × ½ cm/1½ × ¼ in).
• Preheat the vegetable oil in the deep fat fryer.

7 minutes

For the Colada

INGREDIENTS

1 large pineapple
1 vanilla pod
75 g/2½ oz icing sugar
200 ml/7 fl oz double cream
100 ml/4 fl oz Malibu

EQUIPMENT

Sharp knife
Bowl
Whisk
Tall cocktail-style glasses

PRE-PREPARATION

• Peel and core the pineapple and cut it into 1.5-cm/⅔-inch square chunks.
• Split the vanilla pod, scrape out the seeds and add them to the sugar (save the pods and keep them wrapped in cling film for use elsewhere).
• Semi-whip the cream so that it forms ribbons.

5 minutes

Place the processed satay ingredients in a saucepan, cover with the stock and coconut milk, bring to the boil, then turn down to a simmer and cook for 15 minutes.

2 *minutes*

Put the monkfish on the roasting tray, cover with a little of the rosemary oil and season well. Roast on a low shelf in the preheated oven for approximately 7 minutes until spongy – flaky is overcooked.

2 *minutes*

Now sear the beef steaks one at a time on both sides on the hot griddle, then put into the roasting tray ready for the oven.

3 *minutes*

Put the potato fries into the hot vegetable oil and stir well with a slotted spoon (to prevent them sticking together). Keep an eye on the fries and, if necessary, turn down the fat to 140–150°C/ 285–300°F to prevent them browning too much before cooking properly. Remove the monkfish from the oven.

5 *minutes*

Start adding the butter to the reduced wine syrup for the monkfish sauce. Whisk it in a lump at a time to form a creamy smooth sauce. Pass this through a fine sieve into a clean pan, taste and season, add the lemon juice and keep warm. Remove the fries and drain on kitchen paper.

 5 *minutes*

Put the beef in the oven for approximately 7 minutes for rare. Meanwhile, stir the satay sauce and check for seasoning. Add the soy sauce and lemon juice.

2 *minutes*

Blanch the noodles for 3 minutes in boiling water with a little olive oil, then drain through a sieve or colander.

3 *minutes*

Put the monkfish on a small neat pile of noodles and pour over the butter sauce. Garnish with a small sprig of rosemary. Serve.

4 *minutes*

Remove the beef from the oven and keep warm until ready to serve. In the meantime, quickly refry the fries in the hot oil to crisp them. Drain immediately and season well with salt.

 2 *minutes*

Serve the beef with the satay sauce on the side and the fries in a tower on top. Serve with a tomato, rocket and Parmesan salad, if desired.

 2 *minutes*

Pour the Malibu over equal quantities of the pineapple in each glass. Whisk the cream, sugar and vanilla together, and pour this smooth, thick mixture over the top of the pineapple and Malibu. Garnish with a leaf of pineapple.

4 *minutes*

SEAFOOD RISOTTO

MARINATED RIB OF BEEF

with

SWEET POTATO CAKES AND

CANDIED SHALLOTS

FRUIT GRATIN

with

SPARKLING WINE SABAYON

**Total cooking time for 3 courses
approximately 24 minutes and
preparation time 24 minutes**

Right: Fruit Gratin with Sparkling Wine Sabayon

This risotto uses shrimps, prawns, cockles and mussels, which you could substitute with any fresh shellfish. The secret is not what you put in, but what's come most recently from the sea.

Rib of beef is one of the tastiest cuts, and although it can be a little more fatty it does bring a deep flavour to the dish. Marinating it with plenty of garlic, coriander and soy only adds to this, giving it an edge on any beef dish you already know. Rib is also less expensive than sirloin and fillet. You should ask your butcher to give you the rib-eye off the bone rather than rolling too much of the outer flank and tying that to the eye, as this will be too fatty.

I was very tempted to use champagne in the pudding, but to keep costs down opted for a sparkling wine. But if you've got any champagne lying around . . .

For the Risotto

INGREDIENTS

200 g/7 oz shrimps or prawns
575 ml/1 pint fish stock (see page 9)
24 mussels
115 g/4 oz cockles
1 shallot
1 garlic clove
150 ml/5 fl oz dry white wine
175 g/6½ oz arborio (risotto) rice
100 ml/4 fl oz double cream
Salt and freshly ground black pepper
1 tbsp chopped parsley
The juice of 1 lemon

EQUIPMENT

Sharp knife
Deep saucepan
Ladle
Wooden spoon

PRE-PREPARATION

• Prepare the fish stock (see page 9) or alternatively place 150 ml/5 fl oz water, 100 ml/4 fl oz dry wine, a sliced lemon, a bay leaf and seasoning, in a saucepan and simmer for 20 minutes while you complete the other preparation.
• Wash, clean and de-beard the mussels and check the shellfish.
• Finely chop the shallot and crush the garlic.

 10 minutes

For the Beef

INGREDIENTS

for the marinade
½ bottle red cooking wine
1 tsp allspice or mixed spice
2 tbsp soy sauce
2 garlic cloves, crushed
Large bunch fresh coriander
   (or 2 heaped tbsp dried)
Salt and freshly ground black pepper
Olive oil
4 × 225 g/8 oz rib-eye beef steaks
2 large sweet potatoes
Salt and freshly ground black pepper
12 shallots
1 tbsp caster sugar
A little cooking oil
1 Egg yolk

EQUIPMENT

Dish for marinating the beef
Sharp knife
Peeler
Saucepan for the potatoes
Griddle
Saucepan for the shallots
Frying pan for the shallots
Glass bowl for mashing the sweet potato
Potato masher
Baking tray

SEE OVER FOR PRE-PREPARATION

PRE-PREPARATION

- Strip away the fat on the rib steaks so that they don't curl up when they cook.
- Blend together all the marinade ingredients, pour over the beef steaks and allow to marinate for as long as possible.
- Peel and chop the sweet potatoes, cover with cold water, add salt, and bring to the boil and cook until tender, about 15–20 minutes.
- Meanwhile, peel the shallots and boil in a small saucepan until needed and just tender, refresh in cold water.
- Preheat the oven to 200°C/400°F, gas mark 6.

8 *minutes*

For the Fruit Gratin

INGREDIENTS

1 pawpaw
225 g/8 oz strawberries
1 small pineapple
115 g/4 oz raspberries
4 egg yolks
2 dsp warm water
55 g/2 oz caster sugar
100 ml/4 fl oz sparkling wine
4 scoops of vanilla (or other) ice cream

EQUIPMENT

Sharp knife
Saucepan and a glass bowl that will fit over the top (bain marie)
Whisk
Ice cream scoop

PRE-PREPARATION

- Peel the pawpaw, cut in half and remove the seeds.
- Rinse the berries, and slice the strawberries and hull.
- Peel, core and slice the pineapple into small pieces.

6 *minutes*

Start the risotto by sweating the garlic and shallot together in a little oil in a deep saucepan.

1 minute

Add the mussels in their shells, shake the pan and add a little white wine. As the shells open remove the mussels, scoop the flesh out, and reserve.

3 minutes

Add the rice and 2–3 small ladlesful of the stock (or the alternative) to the pan. Stir occasionally.

1 minute

Whilst this is cooking, heat the griddle pan until very hot. Remove the beef from the marinade, sear on both sides, remove and allow to rest.

2 minutes

In a hot frying pan fry the boiled and drained shallots in a little oil with a little caster sugar until they start to colour. Meanwhile, mash the sweet potatoes and add the egg yolk and seasoning. Mould into little cake shapes and fry gently in the hot shallot pan to colour.

3 minutes

Meanwhile, reduce enough beef marinade to act as a sauce in a saucepan until it has a consistency where it will coat the back of a spoon. Also, check the risotto and, if necessary, add a little more fish stock.

1 minute

Bring a saucepan of water to a simmer for the sabayon. Start whisking the egg yolks and warm water together in the glass bowl, add the sugar, put the bowl over the saucepan of water – making sure the water doesn't touch the sides – and continue to whisk.

2 minutes

Put the beef on a baking tray in the oven; cook 5 minutes for rare, 7 minutes for medium rare and so on.

1 minute

Arrange the fruits neatly on the plates. Continue to whisk the egg yolks – now adding the sparkling wine a little at a time.

2 minutes

Check the potato cakes/shallots and remove from the heat if golden brown. The shallots will be ready before the potato cakes. Check the risotto; the rice should be creamy but retain some 'bite', then add the cream, seasoning and the shellfish.

2 minutes

Remove the beef from the oven and allow to rest. Check the sabayon (egg mixture) and taste.

1 minute

Add the parsley and lemon juice to the risotto and serve in small bowls.

1 minute

Serve the beef garnished with the potato cakes and shallots (on each cake) and with some sauce poured over the top.

2 minutes

Pour the Sabayon mixture over the fruits and glaze for 1 minute under a hot grill. Serve with ice cream in the centre.

2 minutes

CRISPY SMOKED CHICKEN SALAD

SADDLE OF VENISON

with

CELERIAC MASH AND CASSIS ONIONS

TIRAMISÙ CHEESECAKE

**Total cooking time for 3 courses
approximately 21 minutes and
preparation time 18 minutes**

The first time I tried crispy smoked chicken like this was in a local Chinese restaurant. I've adapted the recipe, keeping the sweet and sour and cabbage flavours.

Venison with creamy celeriac and sweet onions is another personal favourite. The sauce is more of a dressing using olive oil with shallots and lemon juice to bring a touch more moisture to the dish; the venison and vegetables provide all the flavour.

If you like tiramisù, try this cheesecake recipe; as ever, it's quick, easy and more than delicious.

For the Chicken Salad

INGREDIENTS

450 g/1 lb smoked chicken breasts

A little flour

Salt and freshly ground black pepper

A savoy cabbage (or crisp green cabbage)

1 dessertspoon sesame oil

1 tbsp soft brown sugar

1 tbsp sesame seeds

EQUIPMENT

Wok or frying pan

Sharp knife

Kitchen paper

Plastic spatula (if using a non-stick pan)

PRE-PREPARATION

- Finely shred the cabbage, wash and dry it.
- Cut the chicken breasts into 'julienne' strips the thickness of a pencil and coat with seasoned flour.
- Preheat the wok or frying pan.

5 minutes

For the Venison

INGREDIENTS

800 g/1¾ lb venison saddle steaks, cut into
    4 equal-sized portions

1 celeriac

2 large onions

2 shallots

1 bunch of fresh parsley

Cooking oil

150 ml/5 fl oz crème de cassis (or blackcurrant
    cordial), or to taste

1 tbsp double cream

Freshly grated nutmeg

Salt and freshly ground black pepper

100 ml/4 fl oz olive oil

The juice of 1 lemon

EQUIPMENT

Sharp knife

Saucepan for the celeriac

Frying pan

Roasting tray

Saucepan for the onions

Saucepan for the dressing

Wooden spoon

• Peel and cut the celeriac into 1-cm/½-inch cubes, place in a saucepan, cover with water and cook until tender (usually 10 minutes) as you proceed with the other cooking.

• Peel and slice the onions.

• Peel and finely chop the shallots.

• Chop the parsley

• Preheat the oven to 200°C/400°F, gas mark 6. Preheat a frying pan.

8 minutes

For the Cheesecake

INGREDIENTS

75 g/2½ oz butter (softened) for the base
175 g/6½ oz ginger biscuits
1 tbsp strong black coffee (or concentrate or
  amaretto liqueur)
50 g/2 oz melted butter to grease the mould
225 g/8 oz mascarpone cheese
55 g/2 oz icing sugar
Cocoa for dusting
Grated plain chocolate for decoration (optional)
Tiny amaretti biscuits for decoration (optional)

EQUIPMENT

Food processor
18 cm/7 inch flan tin with removable base
Mixing bowl
Wooden spoon
Whisk
Sieve

PRE-PREPARATION

• Blend the butter and biscuits together in a food processor.

• Mix up the strong coffee and allow to cool completely.

• Lightly grease the flan tin with the butter paper.

5 minutes

SEE OVER FOR METHOD

Pour a little oil into a hot frying pan, seal the venison all over, then place on a roasting tray and roast in the preheated oven for approximately 7–8 minutes for medium rare.

2 *minutes*

Place the sliced onions in a saucepan, cover with the cassis and bring to the boil. Turn down the heat to a simmer and allow the onions to totally absorb the liqueur (approximately 10 minutes).

1 *minute*

Mash the celeriac and add in the cream and a little grated nutmeg using a wooden spoon. Season to taste and keep warm on a low heat.

2 *minutes*

Warm the olive oil with the shallots and add the lemon juice. Set aside and keep warm.

1 *minute*

In the hot wok or frying pan add a little oil and fry the chicken strips so that they turn brown, turning with the spatula. Add the sugar and sesame seeds and cook on a low heat for 2 minutes until crispy.

3 *minutes*

Remove and drain the chicken on kitchen paper. Wipe out the wok, reheat and add a little more oil. Fry the shredded cabbage for 2 minutes and season. Remove the venison from the oven and allow to rest. Remove the onions from the heat, if ready.

3 *minutes*

Mix the mascarpone in a bowl with the sugar and coffee, using a wooden spoon.

1 *minute*

Pack the biscuit base into the bottom and around the sides of the flan ring and cover this with the mascarpone mixture.

2 *minutes*

Dust with sieved cocoa powder and garnish with grated chocolate and Amaretti biscuits, if desired. Refrigerate if not using immediately.

1 *minute*

Put a small mound of the cabbage on a plate and serve the crisp chicken on top.

2 *minutes*

Slice the venison thickly and at an angle into 3–4 pieces per portion and serve with the celeriac. Add the parsley (reserving some for a garnish) to the warm oil and shallot mixture and drizzle a little around the plate.

2 *minutes*

Pile the sweet onions on top and garnish with the remaining parsley.

1 *minute*

Serve the cheesecake with a liqueur glass of chilled amaretto, if desired.

PRAWN PATIA

on

NAN BREAD

PAPRIKA CHICKEN

with

BROWN RICE

POACHED FRESH FIGS

with

ORANGE MUSCAT

**Total cooking time for 3 courses
approximately 24 minutes and
preparation time 26 minutes**

Whenever I go to an Indian restaurant I usually ask for this starter. It's often served on pourri, but nan is so easily bought ready-made and is just as tasty. (You can also make your own nan with normal white bread dough rolled flat and stretched into an oval, brushed with oil and grilled on a baking tray until risen and browned on each side.) The combination of chillies, coriander, garlic, lime and tomatoes in the patia will blow your taste buds in the best possible way!

The chicken and okra with paprika continues the exotic mood, drawing on Moorish and East European traditions.

The fresh figs finished with juices of orange and Muscat wine maintains the Eastern theme to the end. An orange sorbet shouldn't be too hard to buy; you won't have time to run one up in twenty minutes!

Right: Poached Fresh Figs with Orange Muscat

For the Prawns

INGREDIENTS

16 king or tiger prawns (cooked and peeled) or
   450 g/1 lb cooked large peeled prawns
4 fresh chillies (2 red and 2 green)
2 garlic cloves
1 onion
1 large bunch of fresh coriander
Cooking oil
1 dsp coriander seeds
4 plum tomatoes
150ml/5 fl oz dry white wine
4 small individual nan breads, pre-made
   (or follow a standard white bread recipe,
   roll flat, brush with butter and grill so that
   they rise)
The juice of 1 lemon
Salt and freshly ground black pepper
1 tbsp tomato ketchup
1 lime, cut into 4 neat wedges

EQUIPMENT

Sharp knife
Large frying pan or wok
Saucepan
Baking tray

PRE-PREPARATION

• Slice the chillies in half, remove the seeds and
shred finely into thin strips.
• Peel and chop the garlic. Peel and thinly slice the
onion. Chop the coriander.

 6 minutes

For the Chicken

INGREDIENTS

4 chicken breasts, skinless and boneless
   (approx. 175 g/6 oz each)
1 green pepper
2 red peppers
1 onion
2 garlic cloves
150 g/5½ oz basmati brown rice
300 ml/10 fl oz chicken stock
1 tbsp Hungarian paprika
2 red chillies
Light cooking oil
75 ml/3 fl oz dry white wine or sherry
100 ml/4 fl oz double cream
2 medium tomatoes, chopped
Salt and freshly ground black pepper
150 g/5½ oz okra

EQUIPMENT

Sharp knife
Garlic crusher
Sieve
Large ovenproof frying pan with a lid

PRE-PREPARATION

- Preheat the oven to 220°C/425°G, gas mark 7.
- Slice the peppers in half, remove the seeds and chop into quarters.
- Peel and chop the onion. Peel and crush the garlic.
- Wash the rice using a sieve.
- Prepare the chicken stock (see page 8).
- Coat the chicken breasts in the paprika.
- De-seed and chop the chillies and purée with the tomatoes and half the red pepper to a paste. Taste and season if necessary.

15 minutes

For the Figs

INGREDIENTS

12 large fresh figs
150 g/5½ oz caster sugar
150 ml/5 fl oz cold water
100 ml/4 fl oz fresh orange juice
Orange sorbet (optional)
3 tbsp Grand Marnier (or Cointreau)

EQUIPMENT

Saucepan
Ice cream scoop
Bowls for serving

PRE-PREPARATION

- Prepare the sugar syrup by mixing the sugar and water together in a saucepan and heating until the sugar dissolves.
- Wash the figs.

5 minutes

SEE OVER FOR METHOD

Start the chicken by heating a little oil in a frying pan and sweating the onion, garlic and peppers, then add the paprika-coated chicken and seal both sides.

3 *minutes*

Now add the rice and the white wine, reduce for a minute, add the chicken stock, cover with a lid and place in the preheated oven for approximately 15 minutes until the rice is cooked.

2 *minutes*

Start the first course by sweating the onion, garlic and coriander seeds in a little oil in a frying pan until tender, add the chillies and continue to cook.

2 *minutes*

Quarter the tomatoes, put them in a saucepan with the white wine and cook them down until they are soft and mushy, approximately 5 minutes.

1 *minute*

Add the orange juice and figs to the sugar syrup and poach the figs until tender, about 5 minutes.

1 *minute*

Warm the nan bread in the oven on a baking tray.

½ *minute*

Add the prawns to the frying pan with the chillies, and warm through gently. Add the lemon juice to this mixture and season.

2 *minutes*

Remove the tomatoes from the heat, add the tomato ketchup, stir well in. Add the prawns and chilli mixture to this pan and keep on a low simmer.

 2 *minutes*

Remove the figs from the heat, add the Grand Marnier or Cointreau and leave to rest. Scoop out 4 balls of sorbet, if using, and put on a plate on standby, or in the freezer. Check the rice.

2 *minutes*

Mix the coriander into the prawn mixture and serve it on the nan bread garnished with a little wedge of fresh lime and a little coriander. Fry the okra in a clean, hot pan and add the pepper and chilli purée. Cook for 2 minutes.

3 *minutes*

Meanwhile remove the chicken from the oven and check, if cooked, pour in the cream and stir well in. Taste and season, if necessary.

 2 *minutes*

Serve the chicken breasts on a bed of the rice with the peppers and a little of the juices around.

 2 *minutes*

Serve the figs (3 each) in the bowls with the sorbet in the centre and plenty of the sugar syrup poured over.

2 *minutes*

DEEP FRIED GOAT'S CHEESE

with

RED ONION MARMALADE

GUINEA FOWL

with

LIMES AND TARRAGON

FROMAGE FRAIS MOUSSE

with

RASPBERRIES

**Total cooking time for 3 courses
approximately 30 minutes and
preparation time 21 minutes**

Goat's cheese fries very well, staying crisp on the outside while going soft and runny in the centre. The sharp sweet and sour red onion sauce has a marmalade consistency, and together these make up one of my top ten favourite starters.

The fromage frais mousse was adapted from a recipe of my friend Aaron Patterson at Hambleton Manor. We worked together on *Here's One I Made Earlier* for Channel 4, and I stole this from him while he wasn't watching! I hope you don't mind, Aaron; I have adapted it slightly, but I think it's very clever because it's so simple, fresh and light, and ends a rich menu well.

For the Goat's Cheese

4 individual goat's cheeses, weighing
    approximately 60–70 g/2¼–2½ oz
4 tbsp breadcrumbs, made from 4 slices white
    bread
Salt and freshly ground black pepper
2 onions
2 eggs, beaten
200 ml/7 fl oz vegetable oil for deep frying
1 bunch of fresh basil
1 romaine (cos) lettuce
Cooking oil
175ml/6 fl oz red wine
3 tbsp red wine vinegar
55 g/2 oz caster sugar

for the dressing
2 dsp mayonnaise
1 dsp white wine vinegar
1 dsp olive oil

EQUIPMENT

Food processor
Sharp knife
Deep saucepan for frying
Baking tray
Bowl
Deep saucepan for the onions
Slotted spoon

PRE-PREPARATION

• Crumb the bread in a food processor, then
season it.
• Peel and thinly slice the onions.
• Coat the goat's cheese in a little beaten egg and
then dip in the breadcrumbs so that they are
covered completely.
• Mix the mayonnaise, vinegar and olive oil
together for the dressing.
• Wash the lettuce leaves.
• Heat the oil in a deep frying pan to a temperature
of 160°C/325°F.

10 minutes

For the Guinea Fowl

INGREDIENTS

4 breasts of guinea fowl, skin on (you may have
   to buy whole guinea fowl and bone them)
vegetable oil
250 ml/8 fl oz chicken stock
4 limes
4 portions of roasted vegetables (see menu 1),
   optional
150 ml/5 fl oz dry white wine
1 large bunch of tarragon
Salt and freshly ground black pepper
100 ml/4 fl oz double cream
Fresh chervil, to garnish

EQUIPMENT

Frying pan
Sharp knife
Large ovenproof baking dish
Aluminium foil
Saucepan

PRE-PREPARATION

• Preheat the oven to 200°C/400°F, gas mark 6.

• Heat some vegetable oil in a frying pan. Season
the guinea fowl breasts and sear them on both sides
until brown.

• Prepare the chicken stock (see page 8). Slice the
limes thinly.

• Prepare 4 portions of roasted vegetables, menu 1.

• Put the breast of guinea fowl in a baking dish and
cover with the stock, white wine and slices of lime.
Add the tarragon, season, and cover with foil. Bake
in the oven for 20 minutes, as you continue with the
other steps.

4 *minutes* **(not including the vegetables)**

For the Fromage Frais Mousse

INGREDIENTS

300 ml/10 fl oz vanilla fromage frais
100 ml/4 fl oz double cream
2 vanilla pods
125 g/4½ oz icing sugar
250 g/8½ oz fresh raspberries
   (or available soft fruit)
Sprigs of mint, to garnish

EQUIPMENT

Small dariole moulds or ramekins
Cling film
Large mixing bowl
Whisk
Food processor
Sieve

PRE-PREPARATION

• Line the dariole moulds with cling film, ensuring
that there is an overhang.

• Semi-whip the double cream so that it forms
ribbons. Split the vanilla pods, scrape out the seeds
and add to the cream together with 100 g/3½ oz of
the icing sugar, or to taste.

• Add the fromage frais and beat well in.

• Pour into the prepared moulds and refrigerate
while you cook and serve the rest of the meal.

7 *minutes*

SEE OVER FOR METHOD

Right: Fromage Frais Mousse with Raspberries

Drop the coated goat's cheese into the hot oil one at a time and cook until golden brown (usually 2 minutes), remove and place on the baking tray.

8 *minutes*

Roughly chop the lettuce and basil and dress with the mayonnaise dressing. Season.

2 *minutes*

Purée half the raspberries in a food processor with the remaining icing sugar and pass through a fine sieve into a clean bowl.

3 *minutes*

Heat a little oil in a small saucepan and sweat the onions, then add the red wine, vinegar and caster sugar, stir well and cook until the onions turn red and translucent, usually 5–7 minutes.

2 *minutes*

As they cook, take the guinea fowl out of the oven (leave the oven on to heat the goat's cheese) and remove the guinea fowl from the sauce. Pass the sauce through a sieve into a clean saucepan, add the double cream and reduce for 2–3 minutes. Taste and season.

3 *minutes*

Put the goat's cheese into the oven to warm through and meanwhile dress the starter plates with the leaves.

2 *minutes*

Stir the onions and remove from the heat. Place one goat's cheese on top of each pile of salad and the onions on top of each cheese.

3 *minutes*

Serve the guinea fowl with the roasted vegetables (if using) and the sauce around. Garnish with chervil.

2 *minutes*

Turn out the fromage frais mousses and drop the un-puréed raspberries into the coulis to coat them. Neatly place the berries around each mousse and then pour the coulis around. Garnish with mint sprigs.

4 *minutes*

TUMERIC FRIED RED MULLET

and

ROASTED TOMATOES

———

CROSTINI OF PIGEON

with

WILD MUSHROOMS

AND COCOA JUS

———

SIMPLE LEMON MOUSSE

**Total cooking time for 3 courses
approximately 27 minutes and
preparation time around 25 minutes**

The main course here is an adaptation of our crostini of pigeon served at the Pink Geranium. Squab pigeon, if you can get it, is ideal, if more expensive. Squab pigeons have never actually flown and are domesticated, not wild, and so are very tender. They weigh about 450 g/ I lb each, so you'll need one per person. Alternatively, substitute any other game in season, such as grouse, partridge or wild duck.

The light lemon mousse can be served spooned into iced glasses and topped with zest of lemon and a sprig of fresh mint for summer crispness.

For the Red Mullet

INGREDIENTS

2 small red mullet, filleted and pin boned
   (so that you have 4 fillets)
100 g/3½ oz flour
55 g/2 oz turmeric
4 ripe tomatoes (vine if possible)
1 tsp caster sugar
A pinch of salt
Sprigs of fresh dill
150 ml/5 fl oz olive oil
The juice of 1 lime
The juice of 1 orange

EQUIPMENT

Frying pan
Saucepan
Baking tray
Whisk
Palette knife

PRE-PREPARATION

• Coat the fish fillets in a mixture of flour and
turmeric, dust and pat off any excess.
• Heat a frying pan.

2 minutes

For the Crostini

INGREDIENTS

4 whole wood pigeon (or 8 pigeon breasts)
150 ml/5 fl oz chicken stock
3 tbsp port
100 g/3½ oz Puy lentils
100 ml/4 fl oz vegetable stock
A sprig of thyme (or 1 tsp of dried)
150 g/5½ oz leaf spinach
150 ml/5 fl oz vegetable oil
4 slices of wholemeal bread
1 garlic clove
100 g/3½ oz wild mushrooms (assorted)
Olive oil
55 g/2 oz plain bitter chocolate
Salt and freshly ground black pepper

EQUIPMENT

Saucepan
Boning knife
Large pastry cutter
Frying pans
Roasting dish
Kitchen paper
Sharp knife
Whisk

SEE OVER FOR PRE-PREPARATION

151

PRE-PREPARATION

• Preheat the oven to 200°C/400°F, gas mark 6.
• Blend the chicken stock and port and reduce together in a small pan.
• Meanwhile, cover the lentils with the vegetable stock, add the thyme, bring to the boil and cook until the lentils are just tender (approximately 15 minutes) while you proceed with the other cooking.
• Wash and de-stalk the spinach leaves.
• If necessary remove the breasts from the carcass using a boning knife, and season.
• Cut the bread into discs using a pastry cutter.
• Heat both the frying pans.

8 minutes

For the Mousse

INGREDIENTS

Juice and zest of 1 large lemon
100 g/3½ oz brown sugar
55 g/2 oz butter
1 egg
1 egg white
150 ml/5 fl oz double cream

EQUIPMENT

Saucepan and stainless steel bowl (bain marie)
Whisk
Mixing bowls
4 glass dishes

PRE-PREPARATION

• Put the lemon zest, juice and sugar in a stainless steel bowl and add the butter.
• Add the egg, place the bowl over a saucepan of simmering water (ensuring that the water doesn't touch the sides of the bowl) and whisk this mixture for about 15 minutes until thick and creamy. Remove from the heat, allow to cool completely, then chill until needed.

15-20 minutes

In a hot frying pan sear the pigeon breasts, skin side down, turn over and seal the other side. Remove and place on a roasting dish.

2 *minutes*

Pour the vegetable oil into the pan and add the clove of garlic which has just been crushed with one blow from the back of your knife. Now add the discs of bread and fry until golden brown (2 minutes). Remove and drain on kitchen paper.

3 *minutes*

Put the pigeon breasts in the preheated oven and cook for 5 minutes.

½ *minute*

Add the mushrooms to the second frying pan with a dessert spoonful of olive oil and sweat them down for 2–3 minutes.

2 *minutes*

Quarter the tomatoes and place on a baking tray, add the sugar, salt and sprigs of fresh dill, and roast in the oven with the pigeon breasts for 5 minutes.

1 *minute*

Reserve the mushrooms. Fry the fish fillets skin side down until crispy, about 1–2 minutes. Turn over with a palette knife and seal the other side for 1 minute, then remove from the heat.

4 *minutes*

Remove the pigeon from the oven and allow to rest. Spoon some lentils on to the crostini (bread).

1 *minute*

Remove the tomatoes from the oven and place underneath the fillets of mullet. Whisk the olive oil and citrus juices together and spoon a little of this around the fish. This is ready to serve.

3 *minutes*

Slice the pigeon breasts in half horizontally. Quickly pan-fry the spinach and season. Put the spinach on top of the lentils and then the pigeon breasts.

4 *minutes*

Add the chocolate to the stock and whisk in. Taste and season as necessary and serve around the crostini and pigeon.

2 *minutes*

Whisk the egg white for the pudding until stiff, and the cream so that it peaks. Fold the cream and then egg white into the lemon mixture from the fridge. Pour into the glasses or individual dishes and serve.

4 *minutes*

TUNA FISH CAKES

with

ROASTED PIMENTO SALAD

GRIDDLED BREAST OF TURKEY

with

TOMATO AND LIME SALSA

STRAWBERRY
SUMMER PUDDING

**Total cooking time for 3 courses
approximately 28 minutes and
preparation time 28 minutes**

Left: Tuna Fish Cakes with Roasted Pimento Salad

For a fishcake, you don't strictly need to go to the expense of fresh tuna — although if you do, you'll notice the difference. As a main course, my children, Serena and Stephanie, love them, although I don't always add the pimentos (peppers).

We don't generally make much of turkey, despite its year-round abundance; it makes a change from chicken and other poultry, and served like this, with a tangy tomato salsa and the creamy Madeira sauce (for which you can also use medium sherry), it's delicious.

This very quick summer pudding uses only strawberries, and, although I do believe English strawberries in season are the best, since this recipe uses them poached, the year-round varieties mean you can enjoy this dish in winter, too.

For the Fish Cakes

INGREDIENTS

200 g/7 oz can of tuna fish
2 red peppers
2 yellow peppers
2 garlic cloves
Olive oil
Salt and freshly ground black pepper
A bunch of chives
2 large potatoes
2 egg yolks
6 tbsp breadcrumbs (ready made, or process
  4 slices white bread)
Vegetable oil for frying

EQUIPMENT

Sharp knife
Baking tray
Cling film
Peeler
Saucepan
Potato masher
Bowl
Frying pan

PRE-PREPARATION

• Peel and cut the potatoes into 2-cm/¾-inch pieces, put in a saucepan, cover with water, add salt, bring to the boil and cook until tender while you proceed with the other preparation.
• Slice the peppers in half and remove the seeds. Lay the slices on a baking tray, add the garlic cloves, roughly chopped, and cover with olive oil. Season well and either bake or grill until the peppers are soft and tender, about 15 minutes, while you prepare the other courses.
• Chop the chives.
• Keep the peppers covered in the oil and garlic after taking them out of the oven (and, if necessary, top them up with more oil) and cover with cling film until later.

10 minutes

For the Turkey

INGREDIENTS

800 g/1¾ lb turkey breasts cut into
   4 × 200 g/7 oz steaks
A bunch of fresh coriander (or 1 tsp dried)
Olive oil
Salt and freshly ground black pepper
3 large beef tomatoes
1 green chilli
150 ml/5 fl oz chicken stock
100 ml/4 fl oz Madeira (or medium sherry)
The juice of 2 limes
100 ml/4 fl oz double cream

EQUIPMENT

Dish/bowl for the marinade
Saucepan for blanching the tomatoes
Saucepan for the sauce
Griddle
Baking tray
Bowl for the salsa

PRE-PREPARATION

• Preheat the oven to 200°C/400°F, gas mark 6.
• Combine the stock and Madeira and reduce by approximately half.
• Lay the turkey breasts in a dish or bowl, add the coriander and cover with the olive oil. Season well.
• Blanch the tomatoes for 10 seconds each (one at a time) in a saucepan of boiling water, remove and immediately refresh under cold water. Carefully remove the skins.
• Remove chilli seeds and chop finely.
• Heat the griddle.

8 minutes

For the Summer Pudding

INGREDIENTS

400 g/14 oz fresh strawberries
2 tbsp caster sugar
The juice of 1 lemon
1 loaf of brioche
Crème fraîche, to serve
Mint sprigs, to garnish

EQUIPMENT

Small dariole moulds or ramekins
Cling film
Saucepan
Sieve
Bowls
Sharp knife
Rolling pin

PRE-PREPARATION

• Line 4 dariole moulds with cling film, leaving plenty of overhang.
• Put all the strawberries into a saucepan with the sugar and lemon juice, and heat so that the juices flood out.
• Strain these juices through a sieve and save them as the coulis. The strawberries should now be soft and tender, but not stewed.
• Cut 4 slices of brioche, then cut 4 neat circles to fit the bottom of each mould. Remove the crusts and cut out neat and regular 2 cm/¾ inch thick rectangle strips. Roll these flat using a rolling pin.

10 minutes

SEE OVER FOR METHOD

Right: Strawberry Summer Pudding

Remove the turkey from the marinade and briefly griddle so as to mark the breast each side, then allow to rest on the baking tray.

Meanwhile, mash the cooked and drained potatoes with a little olive oil. Mix together equal amounts of fish and potato, season well and add the egg yolks. (If the mix is too wet add a few breadcrumbs.)

2 minutes

Now mould this mixture into small, table tennis ball-sized cakes (allowing 3 per person) and toss in the breadcrumbs to coat.

4 minutes

Heat a little vegetable oil in a frying pan and brown the cakes on both sides on a gentle heat. Keep on a low heat to warm the cakes through.

4 minutes

Put the turkey into the oven and cook for approximately 7–10 minutes. Meanwhile, slice the tomatoes into thin 'julienne'-type strips, mix with the chopped chilli and lime juice, and season well.

3 minutes

Start lining the pudding moulds with the brioche rectangle, putting the circles of brioche at the bottom of each mould. You need to ensure they all fit tightly, using 6–8 slices per mould, and that the rectangles overlap each other.

Fill each mould with the strawberries using the wooden spoon and pour some juice over the brioche itself too, to soak through. Fold over the cling film and refrigerate until needed.

2 minutes

Remove the fish cakes from the pan. Remove the turkey from the oven. Check the stock and Madeira reductions for seasoning and consistency (it should coat the back of a spoon). Add the cream. Continue to reduce for a further 5 minutes, taste and season. Serve.

2 minutes

Put a neat pile of peppers in the centre of each starter plate. Place the cakes on top and drizzle a little olive oil with the chopped chives in around each.

2 minutes

Serve the tomato salsa on the side of the main plate with the griddled turkey next to it. Spoon around a little sauce.

2 minutes

Turn out the summer puddings and pour over a little of the reserved strawberry sauce (coulis). Serve with crème fraîche in a side dish and garnish with mint.

THAI GRILLED
CARAMELISED SCALLOPS

———

ITALIAN RUMP STEAK

with

TOMATO AND BASIL

———

HOT APRICOT
SOUFFLÉ

**Total cooking time for 2 courses
approximately 19 minutes and
preparation time for 3 courses 19 minutes**

Grilled caramelised scallops are absolutely delicious served with rocket leaves and fresh lime. The sugar sweetens and browns them, but leaves them slightly pink in the middle. The rocket leaves give the dish a peppery, crunchy finish. If you can get scallops in their shells, clean and reserve them while cooking, and serve the cooked scallops back in their shells, on top of the leaves.

Follow this with my Italian rump. Served with lots of basil and tomato, it should set your taste buds on fire. This is exciting, full-flavoured food, simply cooked.

The hot apricot soufflé is perhaps the only complicated thing about this whole menu. The base of the soufflé is made by first forming a roux with flour and butter, which helps to hold up the soufflé and give it more depth. For quicker still results, omit the roux and just use the thick purée of apricots; the soufflés won't hold up for so long, but it's a short cut you can use if you can get them to the table quickly!

Right: Italian Rump Steak with Tomato and Basil

For the Scallops

INGREDIENTS

20 king scallops (removed from their shells
 and pre-washed)
Rocket leaves, to garnish
Juice of 2 limes
2 tbsp demerara sugar
Olive oil
Salt and freshly ground black pepper
1 tbsp sherry (or balsamic) vinegar
4 lime wedges, to garnish

EQUIPMENT
Bowl
Baking tray

PRE-PREPARATION
• Wash the rocket leaves and place in a bowl.

2 minutes

For the Rump Steaks

INGREDIENTS

4 rump steaks (weighing approximately
 250 g/8 oz each)
450 g/1 lb red plum tomatoes
2 shallots
2 garlic cloves
170 g/6 oz pasta (tagliatelle), to garnish
Salt and freshly ground black pepper
Olive oil
1 bunch of fresh basil
1 bunch of fresh parsley

EQUIPMENT
Griddle
Sharp knife
Garlic crusher
Saucepan
Roasting tray

PRE-PREPARATION
• Preheat the oven to 200°C/400°F, gas mark 6.
• Skin the tomatoes by blanching in boiling water,
then de-seed and chop.
• Peel and chop the shallots. Crush the garlic and
paste.
• Blanch the pasta for 2–3 minutes in boiling salted
water (you can use the tomato water) with a little
olive oil added.
• Heat the griddle.

7 minutes

For the Soufflé

INGREDIENTS

200 g/7 oz dried apricots

for the syrup
100 ml/4 fl oz water
75 g/2½ oz caster sugar

for the roux
45 g/1½ oz butter
45 g/1½ oz flour
A little milk
4 egg yolks
55 g/2 oz caster sugar

55 g/2 oz butter (softened)
55 g/2 oz caster sugar for coating the
    ramekin dishes
8 egg whites
25 g/1 oz icing sugar, plus extra for dusting

EQUIPMENT

Saucepan for the syrup
Food processor
Saucepan for the roux
Pastry brush
Ramekin dishes
Bowls
Whisk
Baking tray

PRE-PREPARATION

• Make a syrup by dissolving the 75 g/2½ oz caster sugar in the water, then add the apricots and cook for 5 minutes until soft. Purée in a food processor and allow to cool.

• Meanwhile, melt the butter, add the flour, and then the milk, egg yolks and 55 g/2 oz caster sugar. Stir well and cook on a low heat until the mixture leaves the sides of the saucepan.

• Add the puréed apricots, stir well and allow the mixture to cool.

10 minutes

SEE OVER FOR METHOD

Sear the rump steaks on both sides on the griddle, then put on a roasting tray ready for the oven.

3 *minutes*

Heat a little olive oil in the saucepan and sweat the shallots and garlic, but don't colour. Add the tomatoes and cook on a low heat until softened, around 6 minutes. Meanwhile, preheat the grill.

2 *minutes*

Brush the softened butter into and around the insides of the ramekin dishes, and liberally coat with sugar. Chill in refrigerator.

3 *minutes*

Place the scallops on a baking tray, pour over the lime juice, add the sugar, and a sprinkling of olive oil and salt, then grill them until they turn golden brown, usually 4–5 minutes.

2 *minutes*

Make a dressing with 3 tablespoons of the olive oil and the vinegar, pour over the rocket leaves and season. Stir and check the tomato mixture.

1 *minute*

Put the beef in the oven for approximately 5 minutes for rare.

1 *minute*

Finely chop the basil and parsley. Start gently reheating the cooked pasta in a saucepan with a little olive oil and seasoning.

2 *minutes*

Remove the scallops from the grill and serve around the dressed rocket leaves. Season with a little black pepper, and garnish with lime wedges.

2 *minutes*

Add the chopped herbs to the tomato mixture, taste and season. Check the pasta and remove from the heat.

1 *minute*

Remove the beef from the oven and serve with a tower of pasta (twisted in the centre of the plate) and the tomato and herb mixture over part of the beef. Leave the oven on for the soufflés later.

2 *minutes*

When ready for dessert, whisk the egg whites with the icing sugar until they peak, then carefully fold them into the apricot mixture until they have been blended completely. Pour the mixture into the ramekins and place on a baking tray in the centre of the preheated oven to cook for 10–15 minutes.

10 *minutes*

Remove the soufflés, dust with icing sugar, and serve immediately.

2 *minutes*

Right: Hot Apricot Soufflé

ICED TOMATO SOUP

with

BASIL

———

LAMB FILLET PROVENÇAL

with

RÖSTI POTATOES

———

WHITE CHOCOLATE TERRINE

with

SUMMER FRUITS

**Total cooking time for 3 courses
25 minutes and
preparation time 30 minutes
(plus dessert setting time)**

I have used a vegetable stock or nage base for this tomato soup (see page 8). It adds depth of flavour, but if the tomatoes are ripe and full-flavoured it should work just as well without it. They'll need to be ripened on the vine for this.

The little lamb fillets are cuts not often used, but they cook quickly, and are great short cuts to tenderness and flavour. The sauce is a bit like a ratatouille, but a quick one – what I call in the restaurant a *ratatouille minuit*. Good old rösti serves as a base for the lamb and adds a contrasting, crisp texture.

My white chocolate terrine recipe has always been a favourite, and is a straightforward do-ahead dish. You can obviously replace the summer fruits with anything in season, or use frozen berries.

For the Soup

INGREDIENTS

450 g/1 lb ripe tomatoes

1 shallot

600 ml/21 fl oz vegetable stock or nage
   (see page 8)

1 tbsp tomato purée

Chopped fresh basil, to garnish

Salt and freshly ground black pepper

EQUIPMENT

Sharp knife

Food processor

Sieve

Bowl

Ladle

PRE-PREPARATION

• Prepare the vegetable stock or nage.

• Roughly chop the tomatoes. Peel and roughly chop the shallot.

• Chill the soup bowls in the fridge.

5 minutes

For the Lamb

INGREDIENTS

4 lamb fillets

200 ml/7 fl oz lamb stock

100 ml/4 fl oz red wine

1 red pepper

1 green pepper

1 aubergine

2 courgettes

3 garlic cloves

Cooking oil

Salt and freshly ground black pepper

Fresh mint, to garnish

for the rösti

900 g/2 lb potatoes

Salt

1 tsp paprika

Vegetable oil for frying

EQUIPMENT

Peeler

Grater

Saucepan

Griddle

Frying pans

Sharp knife

Palette knife

• Reduce the lamb stock and red wine for the sauce by half its volume as you cook – to a coating consistency.

• Peel and grate the potatoes into a clean cloth, season with salt, and squeeze out the juices. Add the paprika and mix well in.

• Chop (and de-seed) all the vegetables into small ½-cm/¼-inch dice. Peel and crush the garlic.

• Preheat the griddle and frying pans.

10 minutes

For the Terrine

INGREDIENTS
160 g/5¾ oz white chocolate
2 leaves of gelatine
150 ml/5 fl oz double cream
250 g/8½ oz soft fruit (a mixture of strawberries, raspberries, red currants, etc)
55 g/2 oz caster sugar
3 tbsp warm water

EQUIPMENT
Saucepan and stainless steel bowl (bain marie)
Bowls
Small terrine mould or loaf tin (18×10 cm/7×4 in)
Cling film
Whisk
Food processor
Sieve
Ladle

PRE-PREPARATION
• You will need to make the terrine *in advance*. First melt the chocolate in a bowl over a saucepan of simmering water (making sure the water doesn't touch the sides of the bowl). Soak the gelatine in a little cold water.

• Squeeze out the water from the gelatine leaves and add them to the warm white chocolate. Stir well in.

• Line the mould with cling film, leaving an overhang. Lightly whisk the double cream to ribbons.

• Fold the cream into the chocolate, then pour this mixture into the terrine mould. Allow to set for *at least two hours* before serving.

15 minutes *(plus setting time)*

SEE OVER FOR METHOD

In one of the frying pans sweat the diced vegetables in a little oil, keeping them moving all the time. Season well.

Pour a little cooking oil over the lamb and season well. Sear both sides on the griddle, then turn down the heat to cook the centre of each fillet. Leave to cook slowly for 6–7 minutes.

2 *minutes*

In the other frying pan add some vegetable oil and fry the grated potatoes, packing them into the pan with a palette knife so that they will retain the shape of the pan. Cook to a brown colour and then turn over, usually 5 minutes each side.

3 *minutes*

Now blend the tomatoes, stock, shallot and tomato purée in the food processor for the soup. When completely blended, pass through a fine sieve into a clean bowl and chill.
   Remove the vegetables from the heat.

4 *minutes*

Clean the food processor. Put half the soft fruit in the processor with the sugar and the warm water, blend to a purée and pass through a sieve into a clean bowl. Add the remaining fruit to this sauce.

4 *minutes*

Remove first the lamb and then the rosti from the heat. Allow the lamb to rest for 2 minutes. Check on the sauce and season as necessary.

4 *minutes*

Serve the soup in chilled soup bowls, seasoned with salt and pepper and garnished with the basil.

1 *minute*

Having kept them warm until needed, slice each lamb fillet into approximately 5 slices and cut the rosti into neat wedges. Serve the lamb on the rosti, with a little sauce poured over and the vegetables around. Garnish with mint.

Turn out the terrine, cut into 1-cm/½-inch slices and serve with a ladleful of the fruit sauce.

SUSHI OF TUNA OR PRAWNS

with

WASABI

BREAST OF DUCKLING

WITH

GREEN PEPPERCORNS AND

ROASTED MUSHROOMS

APPLE PIE IN FILO PASTRY

with

CRÈME CHANTILLY

**Total cooking time for 3 courses
approximately 16 minutes and
preparation time 20 minutes**

Sushi can easily be adapted into canapés. You could use fresh, raw tuna, or even a king scallop, sliced through thinly and lightly marinated in a little lemon or lime juice with some salt. If raw fish really bothers you, substitute pre-cooked king prawns. The rice used for sushi needs to be sticky, and the sweet white wine vinegar gives it authenticity (sushi actually means 'vinegared rice').

For summer evening entertaining I've often followed these prawns with breast of duckling cooked on the barbecue. Once you've got the hang of these recipes, this is the sort of adaptation I hope you'll become confident with.

Filo apple pie is a clever way of preparing a universal favourite very quickly. It has all the ingredients of a French apple pie, with ground cinnamon and mixed sultanas, but the light, layered pastry crisps up easily in the oven.

Right: Apple Pie in Filo Pastry with Crème Chantilly

For the Tuna

INGREDIENTS

450 g/1 lb fresh tuna loin or peeled king prawns
The juice of 2 limes
150 ml/5 fl oz olive oil
Salt and white pepper
150 g/5½ oz glutinous rice (e.g. long grain)
25 g/1 oz Wasabi mustard
75 g/2½ oz icing sugar
Sprigs of coriander

EQUIPMENT

Dish for the marinade
Saucepan
Whisk
Bowl

PRE-PREPARATION

• Boil the rice in the usual way (with plenty of seasoning) while you proceed with the other preparation, drain to allow to cool in the saucepan so that it sets firmly.
• Mix the lime juice with the olive oil.
• Thinly slice the tuna and season, then marinate it (or the prawns) in the oil and lime juice mixture for as long as you can.

 5 minutes

For the Duck

INGREDIENTS

4 Barbary duck breasts
200 ml/7 fl oz chicken stock
150 ml/5 fl oz red wine
200 g/7 oz large flat (organic) mushrooms
1 garlic clove
100 g/3½ oz can of soft green peppercorns
   (in brine)
Olive oil
Salt and freshly ground black pepper
Chervil sprigs to garnish

EQUIPMENT

Saucepan
Sharp knife
Frying pan
Roasting tray
Palette knife

PRE-PREPARATION

• Place the stock and red wine for the sauce together in a saucepan. Simmer to reduce – by the time you need it, it should be half its volume, and coat the back of a spoon.
• Preheat the oven to 200°C/400°F, gas mark 6.
• Slice the mushrooms in half.
• Season the duck breasts on both sides then pan-sear (skin side down) in a little olive oil so that they are crispy and evenly brown. Turn with a palette knife to sear other side for a few seconds.

 8 minutes

For the Apple Pie

INGREDIENTS

4 cooking apples (weighing approximately
   300 g/10½ oz)
85 g/3 oz caster sugar
150 ml/5 fl oz water
¾ tsp mixed ground spice
½ tsp ground cinnamon
55 g/2 oz sultanas
1 vanilla pod
200 ml/7 fl oz double cream
125 g/4½ oz icing sugar (or to taste)
25 g/1 oz butter, melted
2 sheets of filo pastry

EQUIPMENT

Saucepan
Sharp knife
Whisk
Bowl
Baking dish
Pastry brush

PRE-PREPARATION

• Bring the sugar and water to the boil in a
saucepan for the syrup.
• Meanwhile, peel, core and slice the apples.
• Poach the apples in the syrup until tender (5
minutes), then add the spices, saving ¼ tsp mixed
spice for adding later, and sultanas, stir in and allow
to cool.
• Meanwhile, prepare the crème chantilly as
follows: split the vanilla pods, scrape out the seeds
and add to the cream. Whisk the cream until soft
and thick, then add the icing sugar. Continue to
whisk until the cream peaks.

7 minutes

SEE OVER FOR METHOD

Place the duck breasts skin side down on a roasting tray with the mushrooms. Roughly chop the garlic and sprinkle over the mushrooms. Place in the preheated oven and cook for 10–15 minutes.

2 *minutes*

Meanwhile, mould the cooked rice into 8 neat, small balls (4 cm/1½ inches in diameter) and paste some of the wasabi mustard on each, flattening a little.

2 *minutes*

Put the cooked apples into a suitable baking dish. Brush a little melted butter over one sheet of filo, place the other one on top, then place over the apples. Sprinkle with little more mixed spice, and bake in the oven with the duck for approximately 12 minutes.

3 *minutes*

Proceed to lift the slices of tuna or prawns out of the marinade and arrange 2 thin slices or one prawn around each rice mould.

1 *minute*

Whisk the icing sugar into the marinade. Finely chop the coriander, saving some for garnish, and add this too. If necessary, add a little more lime juice. Taste and season.

2 *minutes*

Check the duck sauce for seasoning and 'coating' consistency, and now add the peppercorns to it.

1 *minute*

Finish the tuna or prawn dish by spooning around a little of the sweetened marinade and garnish with coriander sprigs. This is ready to serve.

1 *minute*

Remove the duck and mushrooms from the oven and allow to rest. The duck may need a few more minutes, cooking if you prefer it not to be too pink.

1 *minute*

Slice the duck breasts thinly and arrange on a plate over the mushrooms. Garnish with chervil and serve with some roasted vegetables, if desired (see menu 1).

2 *minutes*

Remove the apple pie from the oven when cooked and cut into neat wedges. Serve with Chantilly cream and some of the pie's syrupy juices.

1 *minute*

ASPARAGUS AND
LEMON CHICKEN
with
PARMESAN SHAVINGS

———

FISH PIE
with
HERB SALAD

———

NECTARINES MACERATED IN BRANDY
with
ZABAGLIONE

**Total cooking time for 3 courses
approximately 25 minutes and
preparation time 35 minutes**

Excellent as it is with the white meat, if you prepared this salad without the chicken it would make a tasty, tangy vegetarian dish.

The fish pie I have cooked in 10 minutes flat on TV, but it tastes as good as any that require hours of preparation. I often serve it to my children, and as it also freezes excellently, you can always have one in stock!

Nectarines macerated in brandy are another delicious alternative to long-winded puddings. It's a dessert that makes use of a fruit not eaten as much as it should be. What's more, the skin of nectarines doesn't need to be removed, and they absorb the brandy very well. A smart way of presenting them is to fan them around a plate, spoon over the zabaglione (or sabayon) and glaze under a grill or with a blow torch. But serving in a tall glass is a quicker short cut.

For the Lemon Chicken

INGREDIENTS

1 bunch of fresh asparagus
1 chicken breast, weighing approximately
   225 g/8 oz
Juice of 2 lemons
Salt and freshly ground black pepper
Fresh coriander or flat-leaf parsley
75 g/2½ oz caster sugar
100 ml/4 fl oz water
2 lemons, peeled and sliced
Olive oil
Vegetable oil
Fresh Parmesan (optional)

EQUIPMENT

Sharp knife
Bowl
Saucepan for the sugar and water
Saucepan for the asparagus
Griddle

PRE-PREPARATION

• Thinly slice the raw chicken breast into 8 pieces.
Place in a bowl, cover with the lemon juice,
seasoning and coriander and leave to marinate.
• Bring the sugar and water to the boil, add the
slices of lemon, and cook for 10–15 minutes, as you
proceed with the other steps, until the lemon is soft
and tender.
• Trim the asparagus to approximately
12.5 cm/5 inches in length.
• Bring a saucepan of seasoned water to the boil.

10 minutes

For the Fish Pie

INGREDIENTS

225 g/8 oz fresh salmon
225 g/8 oz cod
170 g/6 oz peeled prawns
2 shallots
1 sprig of fresh tarragon
200 ml/7 fl oz double cream
3 tbsp dry white wine
3 large potatoes

For the herb salad
200 g/7½ oz baby spinach leaves
1 bunch of fresh coriander
1 bunch of chopped fresh basil
1 tablespoon balsamic vinegar
1 tablespoon extra virgin olive oil

1 garlic clove
Salt and freshly ground black pepper
25 g/1 oz butter
1 tbs double cream
1 tsp paprika

EQUIPMENT

Sharp knife
Saucepan for the cream
Peeler
Saucepan for the potatoes
4 individual pie dishes (or 1 large dish)
Potato masher
Piping bag

SEE OVER FOR PRE-PREPARATION

181

- Preheat the oven to 200°C/400°F, gas mark 6.
- Peel and chop the shallots. Chop the tarragon.
- Skin and de-bone all of the fish.
- Start to reduce all but a tablespoon of the double cream with the white wine and the shallots and garlic in a small pan. This should become quite thick.
- Peel the potatoes, chop into pieces, cover with water, add salt and boil until they are soft and tender.
- Chop herbs for the salad and combine vinegar and oil for the dressing.

10 minutes

For the Nectarines

INGREDIENTS

4 nectarines
4 egg yolks
100 g/3½ oz caster sugar
150 ml/5 fl oz brandy (or enough to cover)

EQUIPMENT

Saucepan and stainless steel bowl (bain marie)
Whisk
Nectarine/Cherry stoner
Bowl for macerating the nectarines
Tall glasses

PRE-PREPARATION

- Bring a saucepan of water to a simmer, place a stainless steel bowl over the top (ensuring the water doesn't touch the sides of the bowl) place the egg yolks and sugar in the bowl and whisk them until they are creamy, then add a tablespoon of the brandy. Keep whisking until the mixture is thick and foamy (usually 10 minutes). Allow to cool.
- Rinse the nectarines, place in a bowl and cover with the remaining brandy.

15 minutes

SEE OVER FOR METHOD

Left: Fish Pie with Herb Salad

Put the asparagus in the saucepan of boiling water with a little olive oil and cook until tender, usually 2 minutes, remove and refresh under cold water to prevent further cooking.

3 *minutes*

Heat the griddle then sear the slithers of chicken in a little vegetable oil for 2 minutes each side until cooked, remove and allow to rest.

5 *minutes*

Put the salmon and cod together in the reduced double cream (reserve the prawns for the moment) and add the shallots and garlic. Simmer for 2–3 minutes until the fish is just cooked.

3 *minutes*

Now add the prawns and tarragon, stir and taste and season accordingly.

1 *minute*

Remove from the heat and fill the pie dishes (or dish) evenly.

2 *minutes*

Mash the potato, add the butter and the tablespoon of cream, and season. Put into a piping bag and pipe on top of the dishes. Sprinkle with paprika and bake in the oven until the potato browns, usually 5 minutes. Do this shortly before serving with the dressed herb salad.

5 *minutes*

Briefly place the asparagus and chicken on the griddle to heat through, then put the chicken on the serving plates, place the asparagus on top (4 spears per person) and garnish with Parmesan shavings (optional). Dress with some of the cooked lemons and blend some of the lemon juices with a little olive oil to drizzle around and over the chicken and asparagus. Serve garnished with flat-leaf parsley.

4 *minutes*

Divide the nectarines between the 4 glasses. Give the zabaglione a final whisk to peak, and pour over the nectarines.

1 *minute*

SKEWERED TIGER PRAWNS

with

NIÇOISE SALAD

———

STIR-FRIED PORK FILLET

with

SAKÉ AND GARLIC MASHED POTATOES

———

PASSION FRUIT

with

COINTREAU FOOL

**Total cooking time for 3 courses
approximately 20 minutes and
preparation time 27 minutes**

These tiger prawns are superb when barbecued. Marinate them first and possibly pre-grill a little.

The pork fillet dish is essentially a stir-fry, but if you cut the meat into thickish strips they'll stay moist and tender in the middle.

I think you can get away with passion fruit in a dessert even in the depths of winter since by its very nature it's an imported, tropical fruit, but there's no denying that this is a particularly summery pudding.

For the Tiger Prawns

250 g/8½ oz tiger prawns (shell on), allowing
   6 per portion

for the marinade

The juice of 1 lemon
1 garlic clove, crushed
1 red chilli (de-seeded and chopped)
1 tsp whole grain mustard
100 g/3½ oz fresh green beans
12 black olives (stoned)
1 bunch of fresh basil leaves
A selection of salad leaves (e.g. baby lettuce,
   lamb's lettuce, rocket)
150 ml/5 fl oz olive oil
3 tbsp white wine vinegar
Salt and freshly ground black pepper

EQUIPMENT

Bowl for the marinade
Saucepan
Skewers
Baking tray
Bowl for the salad

PRE-PREPARATION

• Mix the ingredients for the marinade and allow
the prawns to sit in the marinade for as long as
possible to take on the flavours.
• Blanch the beans in boiling water, then refresh
immediately in cold water. Mix with olives and basil.
• Preheat the grill.

7 minutes

For the Pork

INGREDIENTS

350 g/12 oz pork fillet
3 large potatoes
2 shallots
3 garlic cloves
Small bunch fresh coriander
200 g/7 oz mushrooms (any variety)
3 tbsp sake
75 ml/4 fl oz dry white wine
1 tbsp soy sauce
Olive oil
Salt and freshly ground black pepper
A pinch of Chinese five spice
3 tbsp double cream
1 dessertspoon clear honey

EQUIPMENT

Saucepan for the potatoes
Sharp knife
Wok or frying pan
Saucepan for the sauce
Potato masher
Small saucepan for the garlic and cream

SEE OVER FOR PRE-PREPARATION

For the Fool

- Peel the potatoes and boil in salted water until tender and soft as you proceed with the other preparation, then drain and reserve.
- Put the sake, wine and soy sauce together in a saucepan and keep on a simmer until it reduces to half its volume, or a coating consistency.
- Peel and chop the shallots and one of the garlic cloves.
- Chop the coriander.
- Slice the mushrooms.
- Cut the pork into 3–4 1 cm/½ inch strips per portion.
- Preheat a wok or frying pan.

15 minutes

INGREDIENTS

12 passion fruits
2 tsp Cointreau
300 ml/10 fl oz double cream, semi-whipped
100 g/3½ oz icing sugar
The juice of 1 lemon
Sprigs of mint

EQUIPMENT

Large bowl/basin
Whisk
Sieve
Glasses (iced from freezer/fridge)

PRE-PREPARATION

- Cut the passion fruits in half and remove the seeds with a spoon.
- Put the basin (bowl) in the fridge with the double cream to keep well chilled.

5 minutes

Pour a little oil into the preheated wok or frying pan and sweat the shallot, the chopped garlic and mushrooms.

3 *minutes*

Now add the strips of pork and stir well. Season and add the Chinese five spice. Fry, stirring as necessary, for 3-5 minutes then lower the heat.

1 *minute*

Skewer the prawns, place on a baking tray, and baste them with the marinade. Grill under a hot grill for 4–5 minutes, basting occasionally.

2 *minutes*

Dress the salad leaves with the olive oil and wine vinegar and season well. Add the olives and French beans.

1 *minute*

Mash the potatoes. Start to reduce the cream with the remaining 2 whole cloves of garlic in a separate saucepan. Add this to the potatoes, stir well in and season.

3 *minutes*

Remove the prawns from the grill and serve on top of a neat pile of bean salad and leaves in the centre of each plate, with some of the hot marinade juices poured over.

3 *minutes*

Pour the soy sauce and saké mixture into the hot wok or frying pan with the pork, add the honey, and reduce a little for 1–2 minutes. Taste, and adjust seasoning if necessary.

2 *minutes*

Serve some mashed potato on to the plates, with some of the pork and spoon some of the juices over. Accompany with roasted vegetables, if desired (see menu 1).

2 *minutes*

For the fool, whisk the (sieved) icing sugar into the double cream with the lemon juice and Cointreau. Fold in the passion fruits, and served in chilled glasses garnished with sprigs of mint.

3 *minutes*

Index